Listen, Sister

LIVE YOUR LIFE AND LEAVE A LEGACY

HOW TO ACHIEVE TIME AND FINANCIAL FREEDOM THROUGH NETWORK MARKETING

DEBBI CODER & WENDI GREEN

Published 2018
Jaquith Creative, Bothell, Washington, USA
Printed in the United States of America

ISBN 978-0-9849082-8-8
22 21 20 19 18   1 2 3 4

Library of Congress Control Number: 2018958233

Also available in e-book and audio book formats. For more information or to order in bulk, contact info@jaquithcreative.com.

Cover artwork by Gloria Feeley
Cover photography by Anna Schroeder
Book design by Nacho Huizar
Bio photos by Deidhra Fahey, Francine Gorton

Scripture quotations marked NIV are taken from the Holy Bible, New International Version, Copyright © 1973, 1978, 1984, 2011 by Biblica, Inc.® Used by permission. All rights reserved worldwide.

Scripture quotations marked NKJV are taken from the New King James Version. Copyright © 1982 by Thomas Nelson, Inc. Used by permission. All rights reserved.

Praise for *Listen, Sister*

Tish Cyrus
Producer and television host; wife to Billy Ray, mother of Brandi, Trace, Miley, Braison, and Noah.

I met Wendi in 2004 at our church in Franklin, Tennessee. We instantaneously become the best of friends, and she became "Aunt Wendi" to my children. When their family decided to adopt from Ethiopia, Miley and I came alongside and helped them financially. Back then their family didn't have a lot of money, but it never mattered. They were still some of the most generous people I'd ever known. The fact they adopted *three* kids blew my mind.

Later, when Wendi told me she had decided to start working in direct sales with Debbi, I was happy for her because I knew she could work from home and be with her five children. But I never imagined how much it would change things for their family. I remember her saying, "I'm just gonna do whatever Debbi tells me to do." Well, I'd say that has proven to be a really good decision.

Here's the best part: Wendi and Debbi are the same quality of people today as they were before they became millionaires. They are hard workers with hearts of gold. If you follow what they did on their road to success—that is, truly *do* what they did—I know you can be successful, too!

Gabriel Sedlak
Network Marketing Leader

One of the strongest indicators of great leaders and great leadership is to take information and run with it; to do it bigger, better, and faster; to make it easier and take it further than those before you. This is the essence of what Debbi and Wendi have done across their company and as an example to the industry at large. You can't take people where you have not been, and you can't give what you do not have. They have *been there*, and they *have the results* to prove it! Whatever they tell you to do, do it!

They have mastered having more income-producing activities and more exposure to opportunities in a shorter amount of time. It's the compression of time frames. What would take years takes months, and what takes months takes only days. Saturation is a myth; timing is a myth. The profound reality is that the last guy in can make more than the first guy in, and that *now* is always the best time to jump in. That is why they have the success they have, and it's why I endearingly call them "animals"!

Jessica Bettencourt
Entrepreneur, Adoption Advocate, Philanthropist, Network Marketer, Million Dollar Earner

Read this book, read every word…you're in for a treat! Wendi Green and Debbi Coder have impacted so many lives with their approach to business and life. They live out their faith in everything they do. They *love* God and they want to help others. They are the real deal! I am blessed beyond measure to call them business partners and friends.

Amy Cassidy
Network Marketing Professional

I have been blessed to be under the business leadership of Debbi and Wendi for nearly five years now. Their words and business ethics and practices helped me transform my new business into the multimillion-dollar machine it is today. And yet, they won't take any credit for it. They point to a God who has been as faithful to them as they have been to Him. The greatest example they have set for myself and my business team is copious generosity. For everything they get, they seem to give it back tenfold. Don't just read this book. Run with it. Use the words as tools to grow yourself as a person and as an entrepreneur. You will be so glad you did!

Dr. Melissa Kuo King
Infectious Diseases Physician

Debbi and Wendi are two of the most generous people I know. I likely would not have met or known them except through this opportunity. A large part of my success in this business is due to their guidance and example of "doing the do." I took their inspiration and training to heart when they challenged us to take action. Debbi and Wendi truly are leading from the front. I have had the privilege of working closely with Debbi and Wendi, and much of my ability to develop an incredible team culture came by watching, learning, emulating, and following what they did. They always kept it simple and made it about building relationships and trust with people. They have such a heart to help people. I am so thankful to be one of the thousands of people they have helped, and even more grateful to pass this blessing on to others as well.

Dr. Panda Korman
Anesthesiologist and Network Marketing Leader

As a physician, I love helping others, and our company has allowed me to do that outside the hospital walls, to include my family, and to make my own hours. I attribute our success to Debbi and Wendi's culture where they focus on helping others first.

JoDee Watkins, RN
Entrepreneur, Owner of JBW Farms & Given Wings Non-Profit, Network Marketer, Million Dollar Earner

Impact by definition means "having a strong effect on someone" and therefore changing them. Debbi and Wendi share in this book the truths they've lived their lives by and how those truths have impacted their families, their businesses, and ultimately you. My hope and prayer for you is that you'll apply something you learn from this book, and like them, you'll impact others for generations to come.

Dedication

When we began working on this book, we never thought the words to follow would be a part of it. But this is where we find ourselves, and so it is with both great sorrow and loving gratitude that we dedicate this book to the memory of our precious mother, Nancy. Our sweet momma was the most loving, caring, hardworking, and generous person we've ever known. She prayed with us, cried with us, and laughed with us. She was always there for us. Always. Everything we are today is because of who she was and our desire to be like her. We believe that because of our faith in Jesus we will be together again one day. She taught us that. We watched her live out what it looks like to leave a legacy of all the things that truly matter in this world. We love you, Mom.

MAY 27, 1941 – AUGUST 7, 2018

Disneyland, April 2018. From left to right: Debbi, Wendi, Mom, Jenni.

Table of Contents

Foreword
by Jenni Hetrick

I am Wendi and Debbi's older sister, so I know them very well! My story took a different turn than my sisters, but it has given me a unique perspective to see their success. In 2001, my husband, our children, and I moved to Southeast Asia to do missions work. At that time, both Wendi and Debbi were stay-at-home moms with young families. When I returned fifteen years later, they had both grown and matured in so many ways. Both had birthed and/or adopted kids since I left, bringing us three sisters to five kids each. I was also amazed to see how they had built incredibly successful businesses that had changed their financial situations and how they were partners in encouraging tens of thousands of people toward their own business success stories.

Their path toward success highlights something this book states over and over: if they can do it, anyone can. I know, because I grew up with them. I've seen them change and grow and work to get to where they are now.

As a kid, Wendi was very outgoing. She was the athlete of the three of us, and she had a "go for it" approach to life. Nothing could stop her. She loved basketball and riding horses. She played guitar, sang, and wrote music, something that later became part of her career. Her music is still so special to me, and it has been comforting in some of life's hardest times.

Debbi is the baby sister in our family. She has always been the cute, blonde-haired, dark-eyed sister with the best tan ever. But she was so shy! When we moved from California to Oklahoma in 1974, our mother decided to give Debbi the "red" room—it had red carpet and red wallpaper—to help draw Debbi out of her shell. Debbi also went to modeling school during high school to help with her confidence. Those things helped make her who she is today: a very confident leader!

I remember when Debbi started posting about this new skincare she was using. I saw her convincing before–and-after pictures. At the time, she told me a bit about it and suggested I should do the business with her, but our missionary organization didn't allow business activity while we were on the field. I became one of those people who scrolled past the posts on Facebook. I even turned off notifications of that type for a while (don't tell Debbi!). It wasn't long before Debbi started making trips with her company that seemed pretty amazing: Napa, San Francisco, Maui.

It was about the time Debbi was making these trips that Wendi realized this business was an answer to her prayers, and she decided she was ready to jump on board. Within a short time, she was making those same business trips. Both girls also earned new cars. They kept telling me about the great incentives, rewards, and bonuses their company offered and how natural it is to build a business by sharing with family and friends because, well, everyone has skin!

Today, I am partnering with them, and I am loving the journey. Every day, I see their amazing passion and commitment to their team. What they write in this book is not theory or ideals. It is what they live, and trust me when I say, it works!

As a big sister, I've always been proud of Wendi and Debbi. That has not changed over the last few years. What has changed is how effective the girls have become in making the world a better place. I have seen firsthand the difference this business has made in their lives and the lives of so many people they have trained and helped. If you know either Wendi or Debbi, you know they get things done. If they find out about a need, they are on top of it, helping however they can. Often they do these things anonymously. That's just who they are.

Seeing God work in and through their lives has been so exciting, and I know it's just the beginning—for them, and for me, and for you.

Jenni Hetrick

Introduction

Why We Wrote This Book

DEBBI

I am the youngest sister in my family (I won't tell you how much older Wendi is than I), but I was the first to start a network marketing business, then Wendi joined me just a year later. I'll tell you more of my story in Chapter One, but let me start out by saying this: *our goal is to help you be more successful in your networking marketing business.*

Both Wendi and I believe with all our hearts that if we can do this, you can too! We aren't rocket scientists or Einstein-level geniuses; we didn't inherit an already-functioning business; and we don't work 120-hour work weeks. We are two relatively normal sisters who *found* an amazing business opportunity, *recognized* it for what it was, and *put in the work* necessary to achieve success. We both started with nothing, and today we are earning seven-figure annual incomes. We want to share with you what we've learned.

I love to make people happy. I am a people-pleaser by nature. That's usually a good thing, but it's not always possible to personally help everyone who has a need. Weekly, if not almost daily, I have people reach out to me and ask, "Debbi, what are you doing to be so successful?" I've even had people offer to pay me to mentor them or to train them and their team. I just don't have the time to train every person who asks me.

After hundreds of training calls, one-on-one calls, and private messages, I decided writing a book would be a good way to help as many people as possible. Now, when someone asks me for help, or if they want to pay me hundreds of dollars for my advice, I can say, "It's all in this book. No secrets!"

If this can help you, that makes me happy!

WENDI

Just like Debbi, I want to help people, but I don't physically have the time to train every person who asks for my advice or who wants to know what my "secret to success" has been. Early on, I responded to every request; but as my team started rapidly growing, it wasn't feasible to help every person who reached out. I decided to limit private training to my own downline team. That was helpful at first, but within two years, my downline exceeded six thousand people! Responding personally even to team members became impossible.

Today my team is over sixty-five thousand, and Debbi's is over eighty thousand. No matter how much we want to help everyone, we can't—at least not in person. This book allows us the opportunity to put something in the hands of those who want to learn from what we've done. Honestly, it feels a little presumptuous putting our thoughts on paper and assuming anyone would be interested in them! But we've had so many people ask us for help that we believe this will be a viable training tool for many.

This book contains more than just *our* stories. It contains the stories (shared with permission) of many of our dearest friends and teammates, people whose lives have become intertwined with ours and who have enriched us in so many ways. I think stories are the most powerful way to communicate, and I hope you find yourself inspired as you read them.

We will also tell you about our strategies, our work philosophy, and our value system—all of which are absolutely essential to our success. But I should warn you up front: it's really not complicated. We aren't going to give you "secrets to success," because there's nothing secret about what we do. You probably already know a lot of the principles we are going to share. But are you *doing* them? That is the question, and that is what we hope our stories can inspire in you: the confidence and faith to *act*; and through action, to achieve success.

One last note. You'll figure this out as we go along, but despite being sisters, we have very distinct personalities and points of view. Rather than trying to write each chapter from a "we" perspective, we decided each of us would address every chapter's topic in our own words. We collaborated on the whole thing, but you'll see sections labelled Debbi and sections labelled Wendi. If you're in a hurry, just read the Wendi sections because they're the best. (Just kidding.) Enjoy!

Chapter 1

Seriously, Listen to Your Sister

"If you wish to influence an individual or a group to embrace a particular value in their daily lives, tell them a compelling story."

Annette Simmons, speaker, storyteller, and author

DEBBI

My story starts with... brown spots.

But before I get to that, let me introduce myself. I have been married to my high school sweetheart, Steve, for thirty-four years and counting. We were those crazy kids who got married right out of high school. I took a job as an administrative assistant and then a mortgage loan processor while Steve attended college and began his career.

We have five children ranging in age from nine to twenty-seven (the four oldest are biological and our youngest is adopted) plus two grandkids with another on the way. To be honest, our fourth child was a big surprise (ok, huge surprise) right before

Steve and I turned forty. At the time, our kids were eleven, thirteen, and fifteen. (We call them the "bigs" now). But after baby number four, we realized we didn't want him to grow up all alone. He needed a buddy, right? And the more we talked and prayed about it, the more we felt called to adopt a child. That's how number five became part of our family. And naturally, we call the two youngest the "littles." But all that is a story for another book. Let's just say our life is as full as it is wonderful!

Now, back to those spots. When I reached my forties, I realized my skin was aging more quickly than it had been, and certainly much faster then I wanted it to happen. And I knew why. I grew up as a little girl in Southern California, and then as a teenager on the lakes of Oklahoma each summer. Now, all that time in the sun was catching up with me. My skin was covered with brown spots.

I didn't think I could fix the problem, so I tried to cover it up. I started using more and more foundation. It quickly became far too thick, heavy, and dark for my olive complexion and blonde hair. To make things worse, it always clumped in those fine lines and creases that had also come along with being in my forties. It was not a good situation. Ever heard the phrase "hot mess"? That was me! But I was desperate to hide that brown-spotted mask, so I continued caking on the foundation. I wouldn't even walk to my mailbox without it. True story! That is how self-conscious I had become.

During the adoption process of our youngest child, I met a lady named Crystal Archie. Crystal and her husband, Michael, were also adopting, and our sons were in the same orphanage in Ethiopia. Crystal and I became fast friends through this adoption bond, all through Facebook.

On Crystal's Facebook page, I noticed she would regularly post before and after pictures of people's skin who were using specific skincare products. Those pictures really caught my eye. The products were created by doctors I had heard of years before through another skincare product, so I knew they were legitimate. I had been loyal to the product I was using for almost eight years, but I wasn't happy with my skin. I knew it was only cleaning my skin, not changing or correcting it. I had also tried many other brands during those eight years, but always with the same result: they cleaned my skin, but they didn't change anything. I was ready to try something new.

One day I decided to reach out to Crystal and try these products she posted about. While we were discussing which regimen I should use for my skin issues, she asked me a simple question: "Debbi, have you considered being a consultant?"

Well, no, I had not thought of being a consultant...not at all! Selling skincare products was not something I could see myself doing. I gracefully told her no.

But then she said, "Oh, okay, I just wanted to ask, because we get a bigger discount."

Those two words—"bigger discount"—got me. I mean, why not? Who doesn't want a bigger discount? I said, "Yes, I'll try that." And just like that, I was a consultant. Now, I had no intention of "working" the business or posting on Facebook like she did. That wasn't on my radar at all. I just wanted to have better skin and get rid of those crazy brown spots, and I wanted to do it as cheaply as possible. I had no idea what was in store!

The products arrived two days later. After using the products just one time, my skin felt better and smoother. And within a few days, my skin was already looking better. My husband, who had never commented on (or probably even noticed) any of my skincare regimens, began to compliment me on my skin. Within six weeks I was able to stop wearing foundation completely, and I have not worn any since. That was over six years ago, and today I have the best skin of my entire adult life.

I did what we all do when we find something we like: I told people. I didn't plan to or try to. But when you discover a delicious restaurant or read a fascinating book, you tell others about it, and that's what I started doing. I posted on Facebook because I wanted all my friends to know about these amazing products that actually do what they say. Some of them contacted me about purchasing the products I was highlighting. I called Crystal to tell her people were wanting to buy these products, and I had no idea what to do.

She said, "Debbi, as a consultant, you have a free website for thirty days. They can order there."

Then some of my friends asked about joining the business with me. Crazy! I was "working" the business and growing a team without even knowing it. I didn't know what I was doing, but I was excited to share. That's what it boils down to, by the way. Just sharing something you believe in and are excited about. Anyone can do that!

That was February 2012. And in March 2012, I walked out to my mailbox (foundation-free... whoop!), and there was my first check. I had no idea what to expect. But when I saw the check, I was blown away. I had earned four figures!

Just by telling others about something I was excited about—in everyday conversations with my friends, my sisters, my husband's friends, people who asked about my skin (and they did!)—I grew a business! People are looking for good products, and they trust a referral from a friend.

I was amazed at what I had earned in my first month! I did the happy dance all the way from the mailbox to my house. I immediately called my husband to tell him how much I got paid. He was truly happy for me and my "cute hobby," as he lovingly called it.

Honestly, I have to give a shout-out to my husband for his support and encouragement during those early days. He was glad I found something I enjoyed doing, and he could see how much fun I was having. And I'm sure the extra income didn't bother him, either! But even though it started out almost as a hobby, Steve never looked down on my business or discouraged my passion. The opposite was true—he cheered me on. And as the business quickly began growing to new levels, he jumped in to help however he could.

Each month my income grew. I can only laugh when I think back on those early days. Crystal would call me and tell me I had been promoted to the next level in our company, and I had no idea what she was talking about. Steve would ask me, "When do you get paid?" and "How much do you get paid?" and I had no clue! My focus was never on that. I had never asked about the compensation plan or payday. I just knew I was sitting on a gold mine, and if I would dig for the gold, I would find it. It wouldn't just fall in my lap—it would require effort and work on my part if I wanted this to get any bigger.

And I did want it to get bigger. It didn't take me long to realize that. I knew these amazing products truly worked. I knew I had something people needed and wanted. I knew they would buy them over and over, since they were consumable. And I knew the creators of the products had integrity, experience, and prior success, so I was proud to represent this brand. They had done it before, and they would do it again, and I would be along for the ride.

> People *are* looking for good products, and they trust a referral from a friend.

That was it! I made the decision to do this. To really "work" this like a business and see what would happen. To intentionally tell people about products that would change their skin. To give people an opportunity to earn some extra income, life-changing income, if they wanted to be a part. How? It's simple. Through posting (oh, the power of social media!), hosting (who doesn't need an excuse to clean their house and enjoy some friends?) and messaging/conversations. But more on that later!

In just five months, I was promoted to the top 2% of the company, both in title and in earnings. In thirteen months, I achieved the free car. And by twenty months, I received the highest title in the company, and I have never gone backward.

That is what excitement, belief, and passion can do. Note that I didn't say "work." Yes, work is important, but you'll naturally work at what you're excited about. And often, it won't even feel like work! On the other hand, if you trudge away at something you hate or don't believe in, chances are you won't be nearly as successful as you would be if you were excited about it. Enthusiasm and sincerity are contagious. They give you a voice, a platform, and credibility. If you only get one thing out of this book, get that!

If you don't try, you will never know. If you do try, you may wildly succeed!

Today, I not only make more money than I ever imagined, but my "cute hobby" allowed Steve to retire from his successful (but stressful) twenty-five-year career in commercial real estate just twenty months after I said yes to that bigger discount. He is now my partner in this business, and we are having a blast working together—when we want, where we want, and how we want. The freedom of time is an incredible blessing.

Plus, we are able to give more than we ever did before, and that makes me so happy! We give to our church, to foundations and ministries we believe in, to adoption programs, and more. We were even able to buy vehicles for some of the drivers in Ethiopia who helped us during our adoption process. We give more in a month than we used to give in a year. It blows my mind! That's really what this is all about. We are blessed to be a blessing!

This has changed our lives, and I am so thankful I didn't overlook this opportunity. It was going to happen with or without me, and I'm happy it is with me!

Now, how about you? Maybe you're just where I was a few years ago, wondering if this is for you. Maybe you want to try something new, but you aren't sure you'll succeed. Take it from me—don't overthink what to do next. If it is a solid business model, a great product (preferably consumable), a reputable company, and something you believe in, why not take a step of faith and work the business with purpose? If you don't try, you will never know. If you do try, you may wildly succeed!

WENDI

My story with this company starts with my sister and those crazy spots. (Thank God for her brown spots... sorry Debbi!) Debbi began making an income because she was talking about a product she loved. She was so excited about the awesome changes in her skin, and she was thrilled she was getting paid to wash her face and tell her friends about it. And because I'm her sister, of course she called me to tell me about this wonderful company and these great products.

To be honest, though, I didn't really care about skincare. I washed my face with whatever bar of soap was in the shower. I had tried fancy skincare products before, but I never felt like they changed my skin for the better, so I always went back to that bar of soap.

In fact, when Debbi talks about those years in the sun and about always being tan, it's a bit of a sore subject for me because I was never, ever tan. I hated lying out in the sun! I used to watch Debbi and her girlfriends tanning by the pool, and I'd think that maybe I'd try it so I could be golden brown like her. But every time I tried, I became a red, striped lobster. It was awful! To this day, Debbi has beautiful bronzed skin and I'm a pasty white mess. (I'm not bitter or anything!)

But on the positive side, I didn't have any visible sun damage, either. I didn't think I needed skincare, and I kept saying no to Debbi's invitations to try the products. But when Debbi called to tell me she had gotten a four-digit check in the mail, that got my attention. I was super impressed.

She knew we needed financial help, and she told me I should become a consultant like her. My background is in music, though. My husband, Brian, and I have both been in the music industry for over thirty years. I told Debbi, "I can write them a song or sing them a jingle, but there's no way I can sell skincare." I told her I was happy she was happy, and I'd send my friends to her for all their skincare needs. When my sister would post a before-and-after picture on Facebook, I'd share it on my page, too, and tell everyone to check out Debbi's website. My friends began reaching out to her to find out about the products.

After that happened a few times, Debbi called me again and said, "Ok, you're acting like a consultant without being a consultant. That's silly. You need to become a consultant for real." Every time she'd get a paycheck, she'd call me to tell me how much she was making—not to brag, but because she knew we needed extra income to make ends meet, and she believed so strongly her company could help.

We definitely needed extra income. In 2011 our family had adopted a sibling set of three from Ethiopia. We went from a family of four to a family of seven overnight. We didn't mean to adopt three kids! We set out to adopt one, and one became twins, and then twins became a call from the agency saying, "Hey, we just found out there's an older sister. What would you like to do?"

Brian and I felt if God wanted us to have three kids, he would make a way—financially, legally, and even emotionally. And he did! But the process wasn't cheap, and caring for a family that had nearly doubled in size stretched our musician incomes to their limits. Brian and I had been receiving royalty checks over the years from a song we had written on a Miley Cyrus album back in the Hannah Montana days, but those checks were fading quickly, and we could barely make ends meet. Meanwhile I was watching Debbi's residual income get bigger and bigger.

Then, through a series of events unrelated to the adoption, 2011 and 2012 turned into the hardest financial years we had ever had. We were really struggling. I found myself saying things to my kids like, "We need to eat everything in the pantry before we can go to the grocery store." Cooper and Gatlin (our two biological children) had never heard that before.

I would see Bennet, Kaleb, and Kali (our three adopted children) huddled over in the corner, speaking a language I couldn't understand, and I could imagine them saying, "What have we gotten ourselves into?" It's funny now, but at the time, it was very difficult.

Our insurance company refused to cover our adopted children for the first three months, so I would take them to the Health Department for their checkups and medical needs. I couldn't afford our regular doctor, but the Health Department worked on a sliding scale, so it became my go-to. I remember many times standing at the counter and signing the kids in as I tried to wipe away the tears streaming down my face. Those early days were overwhelming.

As a family, we had always been the "givers." But now we were the "receivers" of donated bags of clothes and shoes for the kids. While we were deeply grateful for the generosity of our friends, it was also hard to tell the kids we couldn't go shopping for anything new. We never had to ask anyone for financial help, but we also didn't do anything extra for about two years. The only exception was our traditional meal out on Sunday afternoons after church, which had always been a special thing for our family. We didn't want to lose that, so we made a rule we couldn't go to any restaurant that required us to tip, and we could only drink water with our meal. We became regulars at Panera Bread and Chipotle. Honestly, I was just happy to let someone else cook on Sundays!

Then, at the end of 2012, two things happened that really changed things for us. First, I was in Los Angeles with my two older kids who are actors and singers, and I was Skyping with the three youngest, who were back home in Nashville. When I opened my computer, just before the screen turned on, I caught a glimpse of my reflection in the black screen—and I saw my mother's neck! What in the world is happening? I remember thinking. Why do I have my mother's neck? Nothing against my beautiful mother, of course—It just looked like my neck had aged twenty years overnight!

I quickly called Debbi and said I needed something to help me with my pitiful new turkey neck. She told me about a certain skincare regimen the company offered. I started using it, and within about three days, I noticed my neck was feeling firmer and looking much better. People didn't stop me on the street to say, "Oh, my, what a sexy neck you have." But I knew the products had made a big difference in my skin.

The second thing that happened was even more difficult than a sudden case of turkey neck. My husband was scheduled to go on a Christmas tour with the artist he was traveling with, but the night before they were to leave, the tour promoter canceled the whole thing. With that cancelation went our entire income for December.

At that point, I knew I had to do something to help bring in some income for our family. Brian was working as hard as he could, but the instability of the music industry was taking its toll. As I lay in bed that night with my stomach in knots, the story of the old man and the flood came to my mind. Maybe you've heard it.

As the story goes, there's a big storm. Rain is pouring down, there is flooding everywhere, and an old man is trapped in his house by the rising water. He prays to God to save him.

Just then, a neighbor rows by in a canoe. "Get in! I'll take you to safety!"

The old man refuses. "God will save me," he says. The floodwaters rise, and the man is forced up to the top floor of his house.

Then a motorboat comes by, and the captain calls out to the old man. "Get in! I'm here to save you."

> If you're going to say yes, why not give it your best?

The old man replies, "Thank you, but I'm waiting for God to save me."

Finally, the water gets so high the man has to climb out on his roof. A helicopter flies over him with a dangling rope, and a voice shouts out, telling him to grab ahold; but, again, he refuses. "God will save me."

Moments later, he drowns. When he gets to heaven, he asks God, "Why didn't you save me?"

And God says, "I sent a canoe, a motorboat, and a helicopter. What else could you want?"

For the life of me, I couldn't remember where I'd ever heard that story before. But that night, it played out so clearly in my head. I immediately picked up the phone and called my sister. I said, "I don't know if you're a boat or a helicopter, but I think you're supposed to help save us." That ended up being a life-changing phone call.

I told Debbi, "I may not know anything about skincare or direct sales, but I know I'm coachable, and I can learn. And I know if you can do it, I can, too." By this time my sister was making a nice five-digit monthly income. I didn't know if I would have that degree of success, but I knew even an extra five hundred dollars a month would make a world of difference for my family.

Honestly though, from the moment I decided to work the business, I knew I would be successful. I didn't know the level of success I would achieve. I didn't have a dollar amount or a title in my mind. But I knew I would succeed. I simply chose to believe that.

My parents taught me a Scripture verse when I was very young that says, "Whatever you do, work at it with all your heart, as working for the Lord" (Colossians 3:23 niv). I knew just like everything else I did in life, I was going to give this all I had. It was the cloth I was cut from. It was what my parents demonstrated to me my entire childhood as they worked to provide for our family. Both Mom and Dad worked extremely hard and taught us the value of a strong work ethic. Their reasoning was, why say yes if you're not going to really try? I made up my mind in that "yes" moment that I would be successful.

That's what Debbi and I want for you too. We want you to decide to succeed. To say, "If they can do it, I can too." Why not? If you're going to say yes, why not give it your best? I decided not to care what anyone thought of me. I was a musician selling skincare, of all things. So what?

As I watched my sister succeed, I came to understand the gift this business was. I was never embarrassed by it. Not ever. Why should I be? I remember my dad purchasing direct selling products when we were younger, and I had bought products from other multi-level marketing companies as an adult; and never once did I think those companies were weird or manipulative. The structure just felt like good business to me. I liked the products, I used the products, and that was that. It didn't matter to me if I was buying them from an individual person versus a department store. Actually I really loved supporting a person I knew. It never crossed my mind to be bothered in any way by multi-level marketing businesses, so I never figured the people I talked to would be bothered by that either. And if they were, that was their issue, not mine. I just decided to share the gift; and as I did, I began to see the financial blessing very quickly.

In three months I had reached the top 2% of the company. By seven months I had earned a free car and was making a five-digit monthly income. I am grateful to say I have never gone backward in title. Today, I have reached the top tier in our company. I understand and appreciate more than ever the legacy company I am privileged to partner with. I have been blessed to grow a downline team of tens of thousands of consultants over three countries, and I make an incredible six-digit monthly income—more each month than what Brian and I made in 2011, 2012, and 2013 combined. To say this business has changed my family's future is an understatement!

And it's not just my family's future that has changed. I could tell you story after story of people I know and love who are experiencing life-altering financial freedom through direct selling. We have countless professions represented on my team: airline pilots, lawyers, teachers, actors, pastors, realtors, pharmaceutical reps, stay-at-home moms, doctors…you name it, I bet we've got somebody in that field on our team. Why? Because people see the amazing income-earning potential direct selling offers. The success stories are real. People are longing for financial freedom and time freedom, and our business is filled with people who are experiencing the joy of both.

One such person is my precious friend, JoDee Watkins. JoDee was among the first people I reached out to because I just knew she could do well in this channel. She is fun, friendly, confident, and simply one of the best people I know. I wrote her a note to tell her what I was doing and to let her know I was looking for awesome people to join me. I asked her about a particular friend of hers, wondering if she thought she'd be interested as well. JoDee responded that her friend might be interested, and she gave me the friend's email address. But JoDee didn't take the bait and say she was interested.

Soon after that, though, she saw a before-and-after picture I posted on Facebook that caught her eye. She messaged me and said, "Tell me about that picture." We got on the phone and had a great conversation about the company and our products. At the end of the conversation, she promised she would get back to me soon, and she did.

JoDee decided to become a business partner with me because she, too, saw the gift that was in front of her. She believed she could be successful, and she jumped in with both feet. At the time she was a full-time forensic nurse, and her husband, Jonathan, was a police officer. They were raising four children, one with an intellectual disability. (They really need to write a book with their full story —I hope they do!) Today, they have been far more than successful. They have changed not only their lives but countless others.

They were willing to be teachable and do what successful people before them had done. They did whatever I coached them to do and more. When JoDee started, I said, "You'll want to reach out to one hundred people in your first month."

She said, "Nope. I'm going to reach out to two hundred." And she did!

Now they have multiple thousands on their team, and together, they are making giant dreams come true. JoDee and Jonathan both retired from their full-time jobs and began pursuing their goal of building a dog- and horse-training facility where they could employ adults and teens with intellectual disabilities. Today, jbw Farms is up and running, and it's all because they decided to say yes and then do the work required to be successful. I'm so glad they did! They took a twenty-year dream and saw it come to fruition in three years. That is incredible! I couldn't ask for better people to work alongside of, and I'm so blessed to call them business partners and friends.

So what about you? What is your story? Why did you say yes, and are you working hard and giving it everything you have to be successful? If yes, great! Just keep doing that! If not, why not? What's keeping you from achieving the dream?

Throughout this book, we'll be giving you practical ways to work your business so you can be successful. But you have to do the work. No one else can do it for you. I couldn't do the work for JoDee—she had to do it. Debbi couldn't do the work for me—I had to do it. Debbi's friend Crystal couldn't do the work for her—Debbi had to do it. And I promise you, we are all so glad we did! Right in front of you is the canoe, boat, or helicopter you need. Will you climb aboard?

Chapter 2

Nothing Changes
if Nothing Changes

"The most difficult thing is the decision to act, the rest is
merely tenacity. The fears are paper tigers. You can do
anything you decide to do. You can act to change and control
your life; and the procedure, the process, is its own reward."
Amelia Earhart, American aviation pioneer and author

DEBBI

I already told you the story of how I got started, but I want to
emphasize the simple, natural process behind my growth in
this business because it illustrates a key point: success isn't
complicated. It just takes work.

When I started, I didn't even realize I was "working" the
business. I just did what came naturally to me: I shared. I was
excited about a great product that really did what it said, so I
shared it with others. We recommend things all the time—we
just usually don't get paid for it. I was eating (more like devour-
ing) a hamburger the other day while in Dallas, and I posted a
picture about it. I didn't get paid to do it, but I was "advertising"

for that restaurant nonetheless. It's natural to share what we are excited about, believe in, and enjoy.

Soon I decided to share with more people by messaging on Facebook and by email. I made phone calls to friends and family. I talked to my friends at my Bible study group. I told people who came to my house. I wasn't thinking about a business. I was thinking, *These are great products! Everybody needs to use them because they work!* That is how excited I was.

My results were incredible. I earned an astonishing first check, and the next month that grew, and it continued to grow, and it has not stopped growing to this day.

When I brought in new people to my team, I told them what I did. "Do these things. It's just one, two, three. Plant seeds. Keep doing it. Meet new people. Talk to strangers. Follow up. Do it again."

Whether I meant to or not, I created a system of simplicity that really worked. Post. Host. Messages/Conversations. Train other people. And repeat. As I watched others complicate things and not have as much success, I became more convinced than ever that a simple approach is the best approach. People will not do something that makes them feel overwhelmed. It has to stay simple. When you make it hard, it stops people in their tracks. They begin to procrastinate, and the next thing you know, they go MIA.

Now don't get me wrong....my 1-2-3 approach is still *work,* but it is work *anyone* can do if they want to. Let me tell you about my sweet friend, Teresa Lormer. Teresa is a mom of three whom I have known since she was in first grade and I was in third grade. We were neighbors, and she was one of my best friends.

Teresa got into the construction business and became an awesome homebuilder. She was vice-president at her company and very successful in her career for over twenty years. Then the recession hit. They had to start selling things. The boat. The motorcycle. The extra car. Then her husband became ill and could not work. They had to sell their home and move in with her parents. They found themselves considering bankruptcy.

I called her one day during this difficult time, and we discussed the business opportunity that had made such a difference in my own life. She knew a little about it already, since we had talked through the years and she had seen my posts on Facebook. I told her she *could* do it and she *should* do it because "nothing changes if nothing changes."

They needed a change, and fast! She trusted me, so she said she would give it a try. For almost a year after saying yes to joining me, she could only focus on feeding her family, so she didn't work the opportunity very much. Meanwhile the family continued selling off personal effects, but they were barely keeping their heads above water. Teresa and I would chat every now and then. I could tell she wasn't really giving much effort to the business. She had a couple friends who had joined her team, and they both began to grow solid businesses. Because they were doing so well, Teresa was receiving monthly checks; but I knew that amount could have been ten times more if she worked harder and grew her personal team. I believed this could be so life-changing for her if she would just do it.

People will not do something that makes them feel overwhelmed. It has to stay simple.

She called me one day, crying tears of joy, because it was payday in our business, and she was so grateful for the money she received. She said the checks each month were helping them tremendously. It made me happy to hear her joy. And it was then that I straight out told her I was thrilled for them, but that amount could be even bigger if she'd really put her head down and work the business like their lives depended on it—because, truthfully, they did! I told her if she would do the simple things I said, and do them consistently, she wouldn't even recognize her life in a few short years.

Once again she trusted me, and she said she would do it with all her heart. And she did! Today I am so happy for the life she has made. She is completely retired from her construction business and makes more than most people with a forty-year career make. She earned the free car. She built a new house. She gives to a foundation close to her heart in big ways. She is an amazing team leader to a team of thousands, and her team is still growing. And it all happened because she finally *did* it and did it *consistently*! She made the changes she needed to make in order to see the changes she wanted to see. And now she is helping many more do the same thing.

> If you work it like a hobby, it will pay you like a hobby. If you work it like a business, it will pay you like a business.

Just like Teresa, let your yes be yes! In other words, decide now if this is a hobby or if this is something you want to work as a business. If you work it like a hobby, it will pay you like a hobby. If you work it like a business (which means being consistent with daily activity) it will pay you like a business.

Of course there's nothing wrong with having a hobby that builds your "shoe fund" or your "date night fund." If that's what you're looking for, great! But if you want to achieve life-changing financial freedom, it's going to take focus, determination, hard work, and stamina. It's not hard labor, but it is work. It's a decision. It's a commitment.

When I started I made a deal with myself that I was going to do this. I knew watching *The Bachelor* wasn't changing my life. Looking back, who cares who got the rose? I wasted so many hours on something that didn't make my life better. But I knew this business could, if I stayed focused. So I turned off the television. I didn't play *Candy Crush*. If I had fifteen minutes here or an hour there, I didn't play *Words with Friends*. I sent messages! Fifty, a hundred, two hundred—as many as I could to connect with people and start conversations. I sent emails if they weren't on Facebook. I made phone calls. I had get-togethers in my home. And it was fun! It was work, but it was rewarding, fruitful, effective work.

The decision to work instead of waste time completely paid off. Of course I still spent time with my family. But I eliminated things from my life that simply weren't necessary, at least for a time. And my business grew. My team grew.

You must make some sacrifices along the way. Remember, nothing changes if nothing changes. Run hard now, rest later. Work now, play later. Be efficient and effective now, and reap the rewards for decades to come.

And keep in mind, *it takes time*. Rome wasn't built in a day. Starbucks didn't become a world caffeine empire in a week. Little by little, brick by brick, your business will grow. And, just like Teresa, you'll be so glad you *did the work* to make that happen.

WENDI

Whatever Debbi told me to do, I did. I never thought twice about it. She's always been on the bossy side, so I was used to taking orders from her. Just kidding! Sort of. But seriously, what she was doing was obviously working, so I duplicated it.

She told me not to overthink things, but just to start. That was wisdom! Often I see people get stuck in their own heads, trying to think of some way to reinvent the wheel when they don't have to. Our business has a proven system for success, and it's pretty simple. It's not always *easy*, but it's *simple*. It's important not to confuse the two.

Debbi said to message people and connect with them, so I did that. Debbi said to host multiple events each month, so I did that, too. Debbi said to listen to some training calls, and I said, "You betcha." Debbi said to organize some three-way calls with potential team members so I could listen and learn, and I said, "Absolutely." Why wouldn't I? I wasn't about to assume I knew more than her about the business. Of course I didn't. I needed her to help me get started.

But because I invested time into it, I learned the business model quickly. I was out of the gate and running down the track as fast as I could. In my first month, I brought three business partners into the business, although one quit before she ever opened her business kit (it happens to all of us). In my second month, I brought in two more business partners. In my third month, I brought in twelve business partners. All because I was doing exactly what Debbi not only *told* me to do, but what she *showed* me by personal example.

At the end of my third month, I remember calling Debbi and laughing and crying over the phone. I was pouring myself into growing my business and helping the newbies I had brought in, and I was exhausted but so happy. It was a pretty hysterical moment!

Debbi told me I was experiencing momentum and I needed to breathe and enjoy the ride. She was right. The momentum in those early days launched my business like a rocket. That year I was told I was the top recruiter in our company. I had built a really nice five-digit monthly income and was growing at a very high percentage each month.

Momentum is your best friend in this business, but it takes a lot of hard work to get it going—and once you are on that rocket, don't do anything to stop it! Work hard to keep the ride going for as long as you can.

And by the way, if you're always stopping along the way to overthink the system, you will lose momentum. I often find people who want to understand everything before they start. I've never agreed with that. Sam Ausbrooks, a sweet friend and business partner of mine, says, "Say what you know and learn as you go." That's truth! You just have to jump in and start talking to people. You don't have to have all the answers up front. You can find the answers as you go. *Yes*.

Not everyone is willing to work that way, and I've seen it affect people's success. I remember one gal who felt like she had to understand everything about how to advance in levels before she could start. I said, "Just work. You'll figure it out as you're advancing." But that wasn't her "style." She needed to know in order to recruit. Today's she's no longer with the company.

> Make a commitment, take the first step, and work at what your hand finds to do.

When you're growing, things are fun. They are exciting. There is adrenaline. You want to work more. People see it, and they want to join you. That's momentum, and it's healthy. But when you overthink everything and insist on understanding every detail and potential pitfall before you start, you risk never getting out of the starting gate. There's a verse in the Bible, in the book of Ecclesiastes, that says, "Whoever watches the wind will not plant; whoever looks at the clouds will not reap" (Ecclesiastes 11:4 NIV). In other words, the over-pursuit of information can actually be counterproductive! Sure, it's helpful to do your research. I'm not promoting ignorance or irresponsibility. But there will always be risk and unknowns, and if you overthink things, you run the risk of thinking yourself out of a great opportunity. At some point you just need to make a commitment, take the first step, and work at what your hand finds to do.

While I was living in that exhilarated, exhausted place of momentum, I received my third paycheck from the company. I was crazy excited. I had set a goal that may seem silly to some: I really ly wanted to hire a housekeeper, at least once every few weeks. With that paycheck, I had more than enough to make the call.

The day she came, I watched her carry a vacuum up the stairs, clean toilets, dust, sweep, and get on her hands and knees on my kitchen floor (it was *dirty!*), all while carrying a bucket filled with cleaning supplies. As I sat there on my couch, working on my laptop, I kept thinking to myself, "*Now that's* hard." At the end of the day, right before she left, I thanked her profusely for how hard she'd worked to make my house look so nice and clean. Then I asked her how long she'd been working for that company, and she told me the number of years. I asked if her job paid well, and she told me what she was making. It was two dollars above minimum wage. I knew what I was making at that point, and it was far beyond that.

Now there's nothing wrong with cleaning houses for a living, and I don't mean to demean her in any way. She was an amazing worker. But as I reflected on the limitations and labor associated with her (all for relatively little pay), I felt a profound sense of gratitude for the business opportunity that had come my way. I

> Often the changes you want to see are on the other side of changes you need to make.

got on my Facebook team page as soon as she was gone and made a post about how thankful I was for my job and the simplicity of the process. To be able to earn a sizeable income from my home—when, where, how, and why I wanted (and often in my pajamas)—is an incredible blessing!

I mentioned my friend Sam Ausbrooks and her great quote earlier. Let me tell you a little of her story and how her decision to say yes to change literally changed her life. Sam and I were complete strangers when she first reached out to me. She had heard of me through a mutual friend as they were discussing adoption. The friend told Sam about our family and how we'd adopted our kids from Ethiopia. Sam and her husband, Rocky, had decided to adopt, but they were also trying to conceive a biological child. She wrote me on Facebook to ask about our adoption agency because not every agency allows families to adopt while pregnant.

Because Sam and I had no mutual friends on Facebook, however, her message got sent to the dreaded "other" folder, and I didn't see it for three months. When I finally saw it, I messaged her immediately and apologized profusely for seemingly ignoring her. We began messaging back and forth about adoption, and part of our conversation included raising funds to adopt.

I wanted the very best for Sam and her family, and because I believe this business is a gift, I asked her if she'd mind if I told her about it. I shared my story with her, and since at that point I had only been with the company for a couple months, I shared Debbi's story with her as well.

Sam was very kind and listened intently to what I said. She told me she'd think about it over the weekend and let me know on Monday. True to her word, she called me on Monday, and she enrolled on my team. I found out later that right after our call, she was planning to say no. But she took time over the weekend to think and pray about it, and she felt something inside her prompting her take a chance and say yes. She and Rocky believed this opportunity was God's way of blessing them. She jumped in and began to do everything I coached her to do.

Today Sam has reached one of the top levels of our company and, more awesome than that, has brought home *two* sweet kids from Ethiopia and birthed a precious little one too! Their income from this company allowed them to fund their adoptions in full. Within two years, Sam retired from her full-time career as a nurse and Rocky left his full-time job to pursue ministry with their church. They decided to try, and the changes they made changed their lives.

I've seen this happen time after time. Often the changes you want to see are on the other side of changes you need to make!

Chapter 3

#DoYourStuff

"Holding people accountable, rather than
doing it for them, is true leadership."
Lori Bush, former president of Rodan + Fields

DEBBI

Recently we took a group of our top team leaders and performers on an all-expenses-paid, five-star trip to reward them for their hard work. This is an annual trip we organize to celebrate our phenomenal team of incredible leaders, and it's something we look forward to every year. Our team members have worked hard to get to where they are, just as we have, and we love them so much.

This particular trip was to Turks and Caicos, a gorgeous island paradise in the Caribbean. During the day we relaxed, hung out on the beach, ate lunch, or just did whatever anyone wanted to do. Because they are amazing leaders, many of them worked a little bit here and there (while sitting on their balconies overlooking the ocean), but mostly it was R&R and fun. Each night we enjoyed dinner as a group, and we talked about our families, journeys, goals, and, especially, our gratitude.

One particular day we were all sitting together on the beach, talking and learning from one another and brainstorming ways to motivate and encourage our individual teams. We started talking about success and how some people just *do it*—that is, they do what they need to do to succeed—while others don't do it. Suddenly one of the gals shouted out something that pretty much summed it up: "Hashtag...do your stuff!" Only she didn't say "stuff." She said another word, but I won't use it here because Wendi never, ever cusses. (Yes, I am the sister who cusses. But only on special occasions.)

We all laughed hilariously in the moment, but it's so, so true. You just have to #DoYourStuff. Ever since that day on the beach, that phrase (sometimes censored, usually not) has become a mantra in our team. It's our rallying cry when we're making plans; it's our encouragement to one another when someone is tired; and it's our cheer when momentum is strong and pieces are falling into place.

I've noticed when people don't achieve success quickly, they often assume something is wrong. They look for something to fix, change, or blame. Often, however, the only thing that needs fixed is their expectations. True, lasting success is *never* immediate. It takes *work* over *time*.

Our business model works. It's been proven time and time again, so that isn't the issue. Our products work too. They are clinically proven, so they aren't the issue. Our brand, company, doctors, pay structure, and marketing strategies all work. They are not the issue either. The "issue" is simply this: do *you* "do your stuff" or not?

We all have choices to make, and those choices will determine our success or lack of success. *You* have the choice to work on this daily or not. *You* have the choice to host monthly or bimonthly get-togethers or not. *You* have the choice to make phone calls, send messages (hundreds of them!), and post before-and-after pictures or not. These are the things that lead to success when you do them *consistently*. Over time, you will grow a strong business.

I say this to my team often, and it's true: you can't just *wish* for your business to mysteriously grow! There are no magic beans here. You can't just *hope* that somehow you get some amazing "runners" (people who take what you've taught them and reproduce it in others) out of the blue. They don't fall out of the sky! And, although I absolutely believe in the power of prayer, you cannot just *pray* for your business to miraculously retire you! You have to *do*. That is what it boils down to. You have to *do* and *do* and *do* and *do* again. The people who are doing are the ones who will succeed. Their consistency becomes a lifestyle, and eventually their lifestyle produces solid results.

My precious friend Lavonne Pylate is a classic example of someone who achieved amazing success by just "doing her stuff." Lavonne was a very successful hairstylist who owned her own shop for over twenty years and had a large clientele. She realized over time, though, that physically she wouldn't be able to keep doing what she had been doing for twenty more years. Standing all day was taking a toll on her body. Plus she always wore heels. She's very stylish!

> True, lasting success is never immediate. It takes *work* over *time*.

Lavonne saw my posts on Facebook and was curious about the opportunity, so she reached out to me. I told her all about the products and the business, and she joined my team. I knew she was going to be a rock star!

Except...she wasn't. At least not at first. During that first year, there were a lot of "things" that came up. Today she would probably call them excuses, but at the time it was her reality. So she put this new venture on the back burner.

I would call her from time to time to check in. I texted her every so often with little reminders that I was available if she needed anything. She would sweetly reply with a smiley face or "Thank you," but that was it. I did that *every month*—something we laugh about now. "Hey girl! I'm having a meeting at my house if you want to come and bring someone to share the biz with! Or if you can't come, send them anyway, and I'll take care of them for you!" Or, "Hey girl, my checks keep growing! I'd love to help you get yours growing too!"

You are basically running a marketing campaign, only it doesn't cost you anything except time.

I'd get a smiley face in reply (though I'm certain she really wanted to send back the rolling eyes emoji!). This went on for a full year. Then one day she called me and asked if Steve and I could go out to dinner with her and her husband, Greg. I figured it was since we hadn't seen them in a long time.

A few nights later, we went out to eat. She looked me square in the eyes and said, "Okay, I'm ready to do this!"

I knew exactly what she was referring to: her business. I asked, "What made you finally decide to do it?"

"It was the car!" I had received my free car the month before, and that got her attention. I've noticed different people are intrigued by different things: for some it is the paychecks, for others it is the free trips, and for Lavonne it was the car. She continued, "I told Greg, 'If Debbi can earn a free car, so can I! I'm ready!'"

She immediately started *doing her stuff*. She did it every day, over and over, as she focused on growing her business and team. Within three months, she had earned her way to the top 2% of the company. See what can happen when you are so determined to be a *doer*? She set her mind on something and did it. The girl hasn't stopped, either! She's on her way to the very top, and I am proud of her.

You might be wondering, what exactly is the "stuff" you should do? It's not complicated! There are four basic components of success: *posting, hosting, messaging/conversations,* and *training*. We talk a lot about each of these throughout the book because we believe in them! They've worked for us, they've worked for our teams, and they'll work for you.

1. Posting

This refers to social media, of course. We'll talk more about this in Chapter Five, but social media is *powerful*! Therefore, you should be intentional about posting the right things, the right way, as often as possible. In particular we love using Facebook because there are so many tools that help you connect with people and build your team. You can also use Instagram, Twitter, or any other social media platform familiar to you and your prospects.

The goal of posting is to get your message in front of as *many people* as possible as *often* as possible. You are basically running a marketing campaign, only it doesn't cost you anything except time. Only a few years ago, if salespeople wanted to reach a wide audience, they had to pour tons of money into print ads, television commercials, radio spots, billboards, and more. Now all of us have the opportunity to reach a mass audience through the power of social media.

2. Hosting

Hosting refers to organizing events. These can be in your home, in someone else's home, at a restaurant or hotel meeting room, or really anywhere you can gather a few people together and present this business opportunity. There is nothing like a hands-on demonstration of the product you are selling—combined with your personal story of how the products and business have changed *your* life—to overcome objections and misconceptions. If you are starting out, you should schedule multiple events per month. And by "starting out," I mean until you have at least one hundred solid team members in your downline. As your team grows, you should also help team members with their first event or two so they can learn how to do them on their own.

3. Messaging | Conversations

This includes text messages, phone calls, in-person communication, or any other direct form of communication. Whereas posting is more of a general "shotgun" approach to reaching out to people, messaging and conversations are focused and personal. They are about interaction, conversation, and relationship. Because of that you have to be very intentional and wise about how you do this. You are conversing with real people, not numbers, and people are more important than anything. They have needs, fears, dreams, feelings, and opinions. You need to validate those things, but you also need to help them overcome anything that might be holding them back.

It's always a dialogue, not a monologue. That means being

sensitive to their responses and patient with their process. It means listening to where they are right now before trying to sell them on something. When you listen to people, you win trust. You gain a platform to speak into their lives when they are ready.

I always tell new consultants they should start by reaching out to at least one hundred prospects. Many of those won't respond right away, so you need to constantly be on the lookout for additional people you can contact. That means brainstorming your different circles of influence, such as family, school, work, neighborhood, social media, hobbies, church, social events, and clubs. It also means being friendly, meeting new people, and getting their contact information.

> This business isn't complicated. If you keep doing the basics long enough, you'll see success.

4. Training

Training is anything you do that helps your team grow and become more effective. We will talk more about this in a later chapter, but a big part of your job as time goes on is to help make your team more successful. This only makes sense—as they succeed, so will you. But I'm surprised how often people don't train well or don't even train at all.

Training is more about sharing and growing together than anything else. You'll find you learn almost as much from your downline as they learn from you. Different members of your team will have different strategies, insights, abilities, and methods. That's a good thing! There is strength in diversity.

A word of caution: never lose sight of the basics. Your main role as a trainer is not to teach people things they don't know, but to remind people of what they already know and to encourage them to keep doing it. This business isn't complicated. If you keep doing the basics long enough, you'll see success. *Post, host, message, train, repeat.*

Also, make sure you don't over-train. Yes, that's possible! We call this enter*train*ment. Don't watch or listen to training all day, every day. Go out and do what you learn. We provide weekly training on our team page, and I joke with my team they don't need to listen to any more training than that unless it's while they are driving or taking a bath! Don't get caught up in training more than working. That won't grow your business.

WENDI

When I first started working in January 2013, I asked Debbi to tell me what to do, and she did. One of the things she told me was as soon as I had a "warm body who was willing to listen," I should get the person on a three-way call with her so she could tell the prospect about the business and products while I listened and learned. I still remember that phone call because it was the only one I ever did like that. On the next prospect call, I asked Debbi to be on the phone so she could listen to *me* present the business and products and let me know if I was missing anything. After that it was all me. I never asked Debbi to do a three-way call with me again. I had listened, and I had learned.

Debbi attended my first two business events with me, and she spoke, and I watched and learned. Those were the only two events Debbi handled on my behalf. I had it after that.

I was confident because I truly believed the saying, "You can't say the right thing to the wrong person and you can't say the wrong thing to the right person." In other words, when you find the right person, they will respond even if you aren't the greatest motivator or the most polished speaker. But if you have the wrong person, no matter what you say, he or she will never be convinced. I think a huge key to success is learning to identify the *right* people and simply help them understand the opportunity rather than trying to convince the *wrong* people to do something they shouldn't do or won't do anyway.

When I was talking to some of my first recruits, I know I said some things wrong. But that didn't matter in the long run. What really mattered was my enthusiasm for the business, the products, and the possibilities ahead. I had a gift I wanted to give them. I knew I was sitting on a gold mine. And that passion helped me do more than communicate data and details—it helped me build a team of people as passionate and committed as I am to "doing our stuff."

The system for success our company has in place works. Debbi helped me get started, and I believe I've done a good job helping my direct recruits get started. (I hope they would agree!) I did exactly what Debbi did because I could see it worked. I knew the only way to *make* it work was to *do* the work.

My direct business partners who have had the greatest success have done the same thing. We don't do every single thing exactly the same, but it's pretty darn close. They, like me, have learned each person needs to duplicate what successful people before them have done.

People need to do their *own* stuff, by the way. You can't do it for them! In order to have balance in your own business, you can't work other people's businesses for them. This is essential to success because if you're trying to work your own business plus build the businesses of everyone in your downline, you will burn out.

Visualize a tightrope going across Niagara Falls, and you're walking across it. That's hard in itself, right? It's wobbly, you're trying to keep the rope still under your feet, and there's water flying in your face. Now imagine you have people who want you to carry them across. You have people hanging onto both of your arms as you walk. To complicate things further, those

> If you continue to do everything for everybody, nobody will get where they need to go.

people only know how to do what they've seen you do, which is carry people. So now they've got people grabbing onto them, and then those people have people grabbing onto them. Eventually, it's impossible for you to keep walking across the tightrope. You're just stuck there, in the middle of a tightrope above Niagara Falls.

What if you had told those people you can't carry anyone across Niagara Falls, and they have to learn how to walk the tightrope themselves? To paraphrase our hashtag, *#DoYourOwnStuff.* Then that's what they'd teach their people, and those people would teach it to their people after that, and everyone would walk their own tightrope. Each person would learn to find balance and make their way across to the other side. If you can get that visual in your mind, it will really help you.

In the long run it's not good to carry people, and honestly, it's not good to be carried. It's not a sustainable or reproducible way to build a team. People will want you to hold them differently, to be more careful, to keep the water from splashing them. They'll keep asking you if you're almost there yet and how much longer it's going to take. It will completely wear you out! If you continue to do everything for everybody, nobody will get where they need to go. You will stall out in your business and so will your team because people will duplicate what you do. Everyone has to do their own stuff. Period.

When you are doing your own stuff, when you've got momentum and you're growing, you're going to feel tired sometimes. There will be days you wish someone else was carrying *you*! Success takes sacrifice at times, but it's worth it in the long run. If you can hold out during the tough times, things will get easier.

One of my favorite stories about sacrifice and work paying off is my wonderful friend, Gina Payne. Gina and I have been friends a long time, and in the early days of building my business, I would often talk to her about this new business venture and how I thought she'd be an amazing partner. She mostly ignored those conversations. I remember telling Debbi one day, "It's so funny—Gina will talk to me about anything and everything except this business."

But one day Gina's husband, Philip, told her he had seen my post about earning a free car with my company, and he suggested she should call me and talk to me very seriously about the business. At the time Gina was a very successful pharmaceutical rep, but her company had been experiencing some layoffs, so she thought it was a good time to look into other income sources, just in case. After many long discussions and some wise words from my husband, Brian (way to go, Brian!), Gina joined me in business.

And then, kind of like Debbi's friend Lavonne, she went MIA. She bought her consultant kit and disappeared for three months. I learned later Gina thought she had a better way to work the business than our system. Once she realized it wasn't working, she knew she either had to quit or call me, eat a piece of humble pie, and ask for help. Thankfully, she likes pie! I love that girl. On that "back from hiding" call, we talked about duplicating the things that work. In a very short time (after doing what I told her to do, which is what Debbi told me to do), Gina was earning a sizable income that matched her fifteen-year career salary.

I'll never forget the day Gina called me during a season of momentum and sacrifice. She was scheduled to drive three hours to an event in another state, but she was worn out from working all day (yes, she started her new business while still working full time and raising three kids). She was in tears as she questioned whether or not she had enough energy to go to the event and present the business and products. I told her to pull over at the nearest gas station, buy a Coke, set her alarm for fifteen minutes, and just rest. I said, "When the alarm goes off, drink the Coke and start driving." She made it to her event, and she told me afterward it was one of the best events she'd ever been a part of.

Today, Gina is one of the top earners in the company. Long gone are the days of full-time pharmaceutical sales. Instead, because Gina decided to be coachable and #DoHerStuff, and because she was willing to persevere in seasons of sacrifice, she is experiencing time and financial freedom beyond what she ever thought possible.

Those two things—time freedom and financial freedom—are the end result of "doing your stuff." And let me tell you, *they are worth it.* Yes, there is a lot of hard work that goes into building a business. But it's work that has a purpose. It's work that builds a future. Having the flexibility to spend time on what is really important is priceless, and it makes all the sacrifice it takes to get there seem small by comparison.

Recently my dad came from his home in Oklahoma to visit my family in California. Debbi arranged his flights, and I was supposed to handle booking his hotel room while he stayed in

San Diego. Life got a little crazy, and I totally forgot to book the room, so Dad made his own reservations. A couple days before he was set to travel, I realized my oversight and called him in a panic. He assured me all was well and he'd taken care of it. He had booked his rooms at the Holiday Inn Express.

Now there is nothing wrong with the Holiday Inn Express, but when Debbi Coder asks you to make hotel reservations for your dad, she is *not* talking about the Holiday Inn Express. But since Dad had already prepaid his rooms, we kept his reservations there, and I made him promise not to tell Debbi I'd dropped the ball. I sent him money to reimburse the hotel (because the least I could do was pay for it!) and thought our little secret was safe.

> It's not about money—it's about memories.

Well, Dad decided to post a picture on Facebook of the fancy pancake maker the hotel had for their complimentary breakfast, and Debbi knew that was no five-star hotel. Darn it! I was caught.

That part of the story has nothing to do with this chapter—I just thought it was hilarious! But here's my point. During that trip, we were able to do whatever we wanted to do with my dad. I didn't have to ask for time off work, and I didn't have to keep looking at my bank balance to make sure we weren't spending too much. We went wherever we wanted, whenever we wanted. We went sightseeing, we ate out (way too much), and we had a blast. We made memories every day. My kids will always remember those days they got to spend with their grandpa, and my dad had the time of his life with his grandkids.

I only tell you this because there's *freedom* in having that kind of flexibility and security. It's not about money—it's about memories. But it took money to get Dad here, it took money to put gas in the car to drive around town, and it took money to pay for those fun family meals.

I'm so grateful to have the kind of income that allows us to live with incredible time freedom. But that money was earned through a lot of hard work, because I decided to do my stuff. I didn't stumble upon some get-rich-quick scheme. I worked hard, and I worked consistently, and I saw the results.

Growing up, my dad showed me what a work ethic looked like. He worked hard his whole life to provide for our family, and he taught me to be a hard worker.

So Dad, I'm sorry I dropped the ball on the fancy hotel. (Actually, he really doesn't care. Debbi, I'm sorry I dropped the ball on the fancy hotel!). But I'm thankful you got to be here with us and we could spoil you just a little bit. You were the original #DoYourStuff guy, and we are forever grateful!

Chapter 4

It's All in Your Mind

"Dear optimist, pessimist, and realist: While you guys were
busy arguing about the glass of wine, I drank it!
Sincerely, the opportunist!"
Lori Greiner, inventor, QVC host and 'Shark Tank' investor

DEBBI

I learned two things early on in life: *to think for myself* and *to never quit.* They seem simple enough, but it's surprising how many times I've had to remember and rely on those two things.

Growing up, my parents owned a janitorial company. My sisters and I would work for them during summer breaks and holidays to make extra spending money. It was a lot of fun. And yes, Wendi, our older sister Jenni, and I actually cleaned toilets! Eventually, though, we were all promoted to answering the phones and running the front desk.

When people would apply for a job, we would get the application form together. The form was about five pages long, and across the last page, in bold letters, was this title: THINK FOR YOURSELF. This page had ten questions that were all *What would you do?* scenarios. For example, "What would you do if you were cleaning an office and the bathroom sink started overflowing?" Or, "What would you do if you were cleaning a desk and you knocked over a vase and broke it?" I loved it! I enjoyed thinking about how I would respond. My dad created that page, and it was just one of the ways he taught us to think for ourselves.

I have always tried to instill this kind of thinking in my children. I remember being at a doctor's appointment with my daughter, Makenzi, when she was about twelve years old. The receptionist handed me the forms to fill out for Makenzi, but I gave them to her to fill out instead. She got to the address part. Under the heading *Address Line 1*, she put our address. Then she saw the next line, *Address Line 2*. She put her finger on the line, looked at me, and asked, "Mom, what do I put here?"

> When it comes to "doing your stuff," and especially doing it for a long time, emotions are great copilots but lousy drivers.

I smiled and said, "What do you think you put there?"

She smiled back at me, left the line blank, and skipped to the next line, *City*. That was it. I didn't give her the answer. She just had to think about it, and she figured it out on her own. I did that to my kids countless times throughout their growing up years. *What do you think?*

I do the same thing with my team, and through duplication, I have taught my team to do it with their teams. It makes them more efficient, and it also keeps me from having to answer everyone's questions all the time. No one has time to answer that many questions! If we are helping everyone else grow their business, we aren't growing our own; or, we end up stealing from family and personal time, which is contrary to one of the "whys" behind starting this business in the first place.

We have to learn to stop and think before asking. We have to decide to be self-thinkers. And if in doubt, Google it! If you have a question, there's a good chance a lot of other people have the same one, and someone out there has the answer. Often a few minutes of research can answer questions and solve problems you've wondered about for years.

Besides learning to think for yourself, it's important to never quit. It amazes me how many people quit something when they've never given it their all or never even given it a fair chance. To me, it comes down to this: they never really wanted it. They thought by "signing on the dotted line" a ten-thousand-dollar check was going to fall from the sky. Nope. It doesn't work like that. We have to *do* first, then we get the reward. But I've found for many people, if the reward doesn't come within their expected timeframe, or if the obstacles are bigger or scarier than they imagined, they quit.

Our *yes* has to mean *yes*. I say that a lot. It's actually a saying coined by Jesus: "Let your 'Yes' be 'Yes,' and your 'No,' 'No.'" (Matthew 5:37 NKJV). In other words, be a person of your word! If you say yes to something, do what you say you are going to do. Keeping your word should be a core value for everyone; but I've found that for many, it's just doesn't matter that much.

We have to *decide* what we are going to do and stick to it, because feelings come and feelings go. Moods change. We cannot base our actions on our moods. The successful people you see didn't achieve their goals by working hard for a week then taking a month off because they didn't feel like working. They worked based on commitment, regardless of feelings.

When I started in this business, I remember catching a vision of what this could be and making a *conscious decision* to do it. My yes was *yes*—not *sometimes* or *maybe* or *hopefully*. My moods didn't determine my actions; my actions brought stability to my moods. When it comes to "doing your stuff," and especially doing it for a long time, emotions are great copilots but lousy drivers. They are fun to have along for the ride, but don't let them make the decisions!

Actions matter, not just intentions. We have to be *doers*. I tell my team they can dream all day. They can wish upon a star. They can hope and pray. Those things are good—but they must be accompanied by *daily action*.

In fact, my team name is DREAM TEAM: DREAMERS AND DOERS, because dreaming alone isn't enough. You must do. Even on those occasional days of frustration, I am constantly *doing*. Intentions are good, but they won't grow your business. Action is required.

If you find yourself feeling unmotivated, often you just need a change of mindset. You must *believe* in what you are doing. That will motivate you to do more. Ask yourself, *What motivated me to start this business in the first place?*

That dream—the *why*, as I like to call it—should motivate you to continue. If it doesn't, figure out your real why. Maybe it's being able to spend more time at home with your kids. Maybe it's having extra money for vacations. Maybe it's having the funds to be more generous. Maybe it's the thrill of building something that is *new* and *yours*. Maybe it's being able to work with an incredible team of likeminded people.

Whatever your *why* is, put that in front of yourself constantly, maybe on sticky notes all around your home, so you see it and remember to do activity each day to get you closer to your goal. "Never quitting" is a mindset thing. Decide what you want and do it, no matter what your emotions try to say along the way.

We can say things like, "I'm too busy," "I'm too tired," or "It's not working" all day long. But those are just excuses! I say that gently and with compassion because I've been where you are. Sometimes I'm still there! Life can be very full. But you are no busier than the doctor and mom of three, or the RN and mom of four, or the single moms who are on my team. I could list so many more here, but you get the picture. We all have the same number of hours in a day. Just focus. Decide to do it. Turn off the television for a year. I decided to turn off my television for a year over six years ago, and I can tell you this: my life is fuller and better without it. I still haven't turned it back on.

I've had people reach out to me and say, "Debbi, it just isn't working for me! I've done everything you told me to do, and it isn't happening." My first question is always, "How long have you been doing this?" You need to give it time. It won't happen overnight. Give it a year of being consistent.

The second question I ask them is a hard one, but I encourage them to answer it truthfully: "Did you do *everything* I said to do to be successful?" So many times they say they did it, but when we start to talk in more detail, they admit they only did it once or a few times. Or they only sent out ten messages, not hundreds. And they never posted anything. In other words, they didn't really try. They wanted success to happen with no work involved. But no job will work that way! If you have a job and you don't show up, you're going to get fired; and if you don't have a job, you won't receive pay. The same principle applies in a business like ours where you are your own boss. You still have to work if you want to get paid.

You have to decide—which means adopting a mindset—if you want it or not. If you don't decide and don't work, nothing will happen. If you do want it, and if you develop the right mindset, nothing will stop you.

> You have to work if you want to get paid.

WENDI

"Whether you think you *can* or you think you *can't*, you're right." That's been said countless times, and I have no idea who said it first—but he or she hit the nail on the head. Mindset is everything. What you believe really does matter.

As I write this, I'm in the middle of a pretty serious health crisis that started over a year ago. It's been a very rough journey, and there have been a few times along the way when I thought I might even die. I won't bore you with the details, but it started with a toxic reaction to an antibiotic that almost killed me. For real.

It got *worse* before it got better. About four months into being sick, it became very hard to walk, and for several months after that, I could hardly move. I was unable to dress myself, unable to take a bath, unable to move my arms. Honestly, many days I couldn't do too much but lie on the couch.

During the worst season, I remember very vividly wondering if I was going to make it through. But here's the thing—I didn't let myself go there for more than just a minute. I tried to immediately take control of those thoughts and tell myself I would live, not die. I would say, "I am healthy, I am well…I am healthy, I am well." And repeat. And again. It may sound crazy, but I had to keep telling myself that. I needed my brain to believe it, and I needed it to send the right signals to my body so it would fall in line and be healed!

Our brain is an extremely powerful thing. Every single day during those months, I had to tell myself I could get out of bed. I had to make myself do it. I had to believe I was going to be well. Each day (some days only because Brian helped me), I would get up and go from my bed to the couch. If I could muster the strength, I'd walk some "laps" through the house before I sat down. I tried to take a shower every day (you're welcome, family).

If I hadn't made myself think thoughts of life and healing, I don't know where I'd be right now. I'm not saying I'd be dead—although I might be—but I'm sure I would have fallen into a deep depression, at the very least. The pain was excruciating, but because of this experience, I have never been more grateful to be alive. And I continue to believe for complete healing and restoration, since I'm not there yet.

In the midst of dealing with this sickness, I organized a big event here in Los Angeles, where I live. It was Christmas, and I wanted to do a "give back" event. Earlier in the year, I had organized a similar event to provide school supplies for kids in need. This time I wanted to give gift cards for families in need during the holidays. I knew the event would be amazing, and I wanted to be there. Let me rephrase that: I *really, really* wanted to be there! I was scheduled to be one of the speakers.

> The things you really want in life are worth the sacrifice and the extra effort it takes to make them happen.

I decided even if I had to go in a wheelchair, I was going to attend and participate in the event. We sold a thousand tickets, and I was so excited. The day of the event arrived, and I was able to walk, which was a huge blessing. There was a leadership tea at noon, and then the event was to begin at three o'clock. By the time I arrived, I was very tired and pretty wobbly. I didn't look "normal," and when I got up to speak, I had to tell the audience I was dealing with a medical condition. I'm certain the presentation wasn't the best one I've ever done, but I was there, just like I knew I would be; and everyone was so kind and compassionate toward me. It was such a memorable night as the boxes filled up with gift cards and we were able to give back to our community. It was worth being tired. It was worth having to stay in bed the next day. The things you really want in life are worth the sacrifice and the extra effort it takes to make them happen. So often it comes down to simply *believing* you can do something.

There's no better example of this than a sweet business partner of ours named Teisha Simmons, who is a consultant in the top 2% of our company. Teisha is paralyzed from the chest down, with very limited movement in her arms and no use of her hands or legs. If there was ever anyone who had an excuse not to succeed, it would be Teisha. But she did just the opposite. She told herself she would be successful, and she set her mind to it.

When Teisha tells her story, she talks specifically about changing her thought process and, as a result, changing her life. When Teisha heard about this business from a friend, she was working a full-time job, parenting a teenager, and suffering chronic pain. She decided to do the work her sponsor told her to do (which was the same work Debbi and I were both doing). In less than a year, Teisha was able to quit her full-time job because of the residual income she was making. Today, she is so grateful for the gift of time she has received simply because she set her mind to succeed and did the work it took to accomplish her goals.

Your mindset matters in everything you do.

I told you my story and Teisha's story to say this: *your mindset matters in everything you do*. It matters in your health, and it matters in your business—big time. You will either fill your mind with thoughts of success, or you will fill it with thoughts of failure. Sure, there are a hundred different reasons why you could fail. But there are also a hundred different reasons why you could succeed. Think on those things!

You have to believe you have what it takes to be successful. As I said earlier, when I first started, I *knew* I would be successful. I didn't know what level of success I would obtain, but I knew I'd have success. At that time, five hundred dollars a month would have been success, because it would have put groceries on our table. I had watched Debbi succeed, and I told myself I could do that, too. I planted that seed in my head from day one, and I just kept watering it.

I wasn't arrogant. I just knew if I worked hard, I'd be successful. I had seen that my entire life. When I was growing up, I always wanted to be a singer and songwriter. When I was fourteen years old, I started writing my own songs. And yes, I sang them for anyone who came to our house!

After I graduated from college, I took a job at a radio station in Austin, Texas. One day the owner of a record label came to the station, and I asked him if he knew anyone who could produce a recording of my original songs for me because I wanted to give them to my family for Christmas. He took my very rough demo tape with him that day. Thankfully he really liked what he heard, and he ended up signing me to his record label. (He hired Brian to produce my record, and that's how we met!)

After doing one album with that label, I decided I wanted to put together a trio, because I had grown up in a musical family and loved the group dynamic. I recruited two other friends and we became a trio. I left my first label, moved to Nashville, and began working hard to write songs, sing around town, and pitch our group in order to get another label deal.

The three of us all worked at the same company, and every day during our breaks and lunchtime, we would meet in the conference room and practice. People would stand outside the door and listen to us working on our songs. Pretty soon some of them started asking us if we'd come sing at their churches.

Slowly but surely we started doing gigs around town.

One day, after the head of a record label heard us sing, I got a call asking if I'd be interested in a songwriting contract. I said, "No, but I'd love a record deal for my trio." The next week, we were in his office working out the contract details.

None of that would have been possible without the countless hours of hard work that went into those songs and demo tapes, and none of it would have been possible had I not believed we could be successful. I *knew* it was going to happen. I didn't know when it would come, how it would happen, or exactly what it would look like, but I knew we would succeed if we were willing to work.

Here's the kicker. When I went back for my ten-year high school reunion, the organizers pulled out the "future" papers we had written all those years ago and read them to the group. Mine said, "In ten years, I will be married and have two kids. I will be a singer/songwriter and will be singing in churches all across the country."

What do you believe about yourself? What are you telling yourself? Wake up every day and say, "I can, and I will." And then, do it!

Chapter 5

Cupcakes and Rainbows

"I'm going to make everything around
me beautiful. That will be my life."
*Elsie De Wolfe, author and first professional
interior designer in America*

"For every sale you miss because you were too
enthusiastic, you'll miss a hundred because
you weren't enthusiastic enough."
*Zig Ziglar, author, salesman,
and motivational speaker*

DEBBI

S ome people say I am all "cupcakes and rainbows." I would
have to agree, and I make no apologies for it! This is one of
my favorite things to talk about, because I think it is a *huge*
part of growing a business. I'd rather be cupcakes and rainbows
than gloom and doom! I remember several years ago, when I
was at our corporate office for my first visit, someone from corporate walked over to me and said, "Oh my gosh, Debbi, you
really do ooze with enthusiasm!"

My first thought was, *Ooze? That's a weird way to describe me!* But you know what? I like it! I'll take that too. I love that people notice I "ooze" with enthusiasm. His comment inspired me to continue being excited, enthusiastic, and positive. The bottom line is, if you are not excited and passionate about what you are doing or the product you are sharing, don't kid yourself. No one who's listening to you will be excited about it, either. You probably won't have too many customers or partners join you if you can't say, "I absolutely *love* this stuff, and you will, too!" People can tell if you mean it or not. Find a way to get excited and passionate about what you are doing. And if you can't, find a new product you *are* passionate about!

If you tend to be a bit monotone when you talk to people about your business, add some excitement in your voice. You need to sound happy, and you need to *smile*! Smiling makes a huge difference.

When writing, remember people can't hear your tone of voice, so go a little crazy with what you write. Use CAPS FOR EMPHASIS. Add a few "hahas" and lots of exclamation points!!! Learn the fine art of emojis ☺. Throw in some Facebook stickers and GIFS.

No matter what I write or post, it's always full of highlights and fun. Yes, it's messy. But it's real, it's passionate, and it's me. I'd rather be messy and authentic than professional and cold. I always want people to *see* my excitement, even though they can't hear my voice.

I remember doing this on my team Facebook page in the beginning, and I had to explain to my team that when I use all caps it just means I AM EXCITED, not that I'm yelling at them. I still get a passive-aggressive jab about it once in a while, but I don't care! I want people to *hear* and *see* my excitement!

Very quickly, I started seeing many of my team also begin using caps, exclamation points, emojis, and stickers. I love it!

Several people have messaged me over the last few years and said doing this made all the difference in their private messages and conversations. More recently, those awesome animated GIFS have joined the fun. If something that simple and easy to use can make people smile and laugh out loud, then we should *all* be doing it.

Texting and typing can be misunderstood, so the more smiley faces, the better. In fact I told my assistant, Marny Klump, that part of her job for me was to use emojis when communicating with the team because that's who *I* am, and since she represents me, I want people to "feel the love" when they connect with her. (I think she likes using them now!)

> Sometimes people just need a little push to get motivated.

You better believe I *ooze* with enthusiasm. It's so much fun to be happy and spread joy! I work hard to create "cupcakes and rainbows" on my team pages. Why? Because those pages are basically our office. (Side note: it's so awesome to be able to be at "the office" while sitting on your couch at home in your pajamas and slippers with your coffee each morning. It's the best!) Just like someone would organize and decorate a physical office to reflect the goals, spirit, and enthusiasm of the team, I want my online office to also reflect those things. My business is not just a hobby, so of course I "go to the office" every day, and I want my team to know I am there by what I post.

My team pages are a place of constant support, motivation, and camaraderie. I do fun team challenges and incentives weekly, sometimes several per week, and my team eats them up. (See the "Team Resources" section for some examples.) Sometimes people just need a little push to get motivated. I find a lot of people don't know *how* to be self-starters. It's not my job to give them a daily to-do list (or drag them to work), but I love encouraging them. Often that's all they need. After doing just a few challenges, it's amazing how many people realize the incredible reward that will be theirs just by *doing*. It's changed people by helping them learn how to do the daily activity that is required to grow a strong business.

I love giving, so the prizes I give away are things I think about and enjoy blessing them with: Louis Vuitton bags, jewelry, home decor items, adorable tea towels (they make the kitchen seem so much happier!), fun graphic tee shirts, and even Uggs. And of course, cash prizes, too. Just fun stuff to make people smile. Little things like this make such a big difference in the culture of a team. It's a practical way to show appreciation and reward good actions. And even better, this culture is then duplicated by the team, and it spreads from leader to leader. Great leaders always help develop more great leaders.

Sometimes people just need to see it in action. That's why you can't just *tell* people what to do. They need to *see* you doing it. I host live weekly team trainings on my main team page. Some of my top leaders and I take turns doing these trainings. It is so inspiring to hear these leaders train with excitement! It's like cupcakes and rainbows each time we hear a training. Their stories are incredible, and so are they. All of us are so grateful to be on this team with so many top leaders and earners in the company.

> Don't give negative things too much attention. They don't deserve it.

I was doing one of these trainings not too long ago, and I was talking about how especially hard I worked in the beginning of my business: hosting in-home meetings (I call them get-togethers), attending corporate events, helping my team with their own events, having coffee dates and dinner dates, and doing everything I could to share this business with others. During the live training, I showed my team the calendars (yes, I still have those paper calendars!) from my first three years in business. Each business event was highlighted on the calendar in dark green. And guess what? Each and every month had ten to twelve big, bold green circles showing the events I either held personally or helped my team with. It was that way every month for three years straight. Each year had fewer events that I held and more events that I helped others lead, which is the beauty of building strong.

I still do events, though—even now. I don't just tell my team events work, I *show* them they work. I show them how I did it and how it helped me, and I show them how I continue to do them. When they see that, it creates excitement, and that excitement (and the work it produces) is duplicated by others on the team.

You will always attract others like you. If you are excited, hard-working, positive, and committed, you will attract a team with those same traits. The reason I've attracted so many "enthusiasm-oozers" is because I created a team that is positive. I demanded that from anyone who came on my team, and I am so glad I did! I have the most amazing team: a team full of enthusiasm, a team that looks for the cupcakes and rainbows around them, a team that others want to be a part of. That is why my team is over eighty thousand as I write this, and it's growing each month. And even better than that, I *truly love* the people I work with.

Of course, if I am being totally transparent (which I always am!), there will be those few who just want to be miserable and always involved in drama. I say those people just need some extra love. Extra cupcakes and rainbows! I'll "emoji" them until they smile!

But seriously, who do you want to work with? A bunch of negative, "blah" people who can't find anything to be happy about and who gripe more than they are thankful? Or those who bring cupcakes and rainbows wherever they go? Sure there are times of frustration, but we don't have to emphasize that. We emphasize the *good*! We emphasize the *happy*! We deal with the yucky things privately and quickly and then move on. We don't camp out there or give those things too much attention. They don't deserve it.

When someone tells me this business and team have *changed* who they are from the inside out, that is one of the best things I can hear. I've had numerous people tell me that even if they never made another dime in their business, just being part of something so good and positive has changed their lives. *I love that!*

I am thinking of one lady in particular, a team member of mine who experienced genuine change as a result of being in a positive team environment. In the beginning, she was constantly negative, pessimistic about everything, and always complaining. I think "cantankerous" would be an accurate word to describe her. But not anymore! She has become a much happier person in general. She told me even her family has noticed. There is joy on her face now, and she has a "pep in her step" that wasn't there before. She said it was all from what she learned being on my team. It makes me tear up every time I think about it. Wow! Life changing, indeed.

One last story. Recently, Wendi and I hosted an event together. It was a night to not only celebrate the success of some of the top achievers on our team, but to give back to a foundation we love to support. At the event, Wendi spoke with a gal on the team named Holley Kuhn. Holley joined my team over five years ago, and I've had the privilege of mentoring "Holley-girl," as I call her, since then. We've become dear, sweet friends.

Holley is one of the most positive people Wendi and I have ever known. She is *constantly* encouraging and cheering others on to greatness. She has a true gift of encouragement. I have seen countless uplifting, positive comments she has made on other team members' posts. She is amazing!

At this event we hosted, Wendi wanted to let Holley know how much she appreciated this about her. She made a point of giving Holley a big hug, and she told her how much her encouraging words always inspired Wendi. I've told her the same thing more times than I can count. It's something you can't help but notice and commend.

After the event Holley sent a note to Wendi to thank her for encouraging *her* that night. She said she had gone through a really tough year, and she felt like her world was caving in. Because Holley is a close friend of mine, I was aware of some of what she was going through. But it was a *total* surprise to Wendi. Why? Because you couldn't have known it by looking at Holley—she never stopped encouraging others, regardless of what she was going through personally. I told you, she's amazing.

Here is what I want you to see in this story, though. Encouragement is a two-way street. Even Holley, the biggest cheerleader, needed to be encouraged and loved on. When Wendi, a top leader in our company who doesn't know her that well, put her arms around her and told her she was inspired by her, it made Holley feel so loved! Holley told Wendi she felt like God used her at that moment, even though Wendi didn't know it.

All Wendi knew was what she had seen on Facebook: sweet, positive words of affirmation toward everyone Holley came in contact with. It would have been completely understandable for Holley to be broken down after her losses, but she remained joyful in her circumstances, and that is what people saw. It's no wonder she is so successful. She is a bright light for others! Yes, her life had been hard recently, just like all of our lives can be hard at times. But she chose to maintain a positive attitude.

I always say we must try to find the rainbow in the storm, but we should also try to help others find the rainbow, too. Even when we hit bumpy roads in our business or life in general, we should hold on to the good and remain positive. That's what Holley does. It's what Wendi does. It's what I strive to do and lead others to do, and I hope you do it, too!

WENDI

Deciding to duplicate Debbi's "cupcakes and rainbows" attitude is really important for your relationships with both your customers and your business partners. Potential customers and business partners will be drawn to your positive, "glass-half-full" attitude. Plus, your current customers will be grateful for it, and your current business partners will be much more likely to achieve success if their leader has a positive attitude. Nobody wants to follow a "Negative Nellie." People want to *enjoy* what they're doing.

Toward the beginning of her journey, Debbi made a rule on her team page: no negativity. If someone had an issue, they were to discuss it with their sponsor, but they were not to post about it on the team page. This made total sense to me, so I did the same on my team page. In this business we are constantly adding new people to our private team pages. It would be unfair and demotivating (and also not good business sense) for a newbie to come across negativity and complaining the first time they visit the page. If it was my newbie, I wouldn't want that; and if it was your newbie, you wouldn't want that, either. Thus, the rule.

Sadly, negativity spreads like wildfire. If someone posts their disappointment in a product or a customer service situation, immediately you get the "chimer-inners," and the thread grows with negative comments. It's not like people are *trying* to grow the negativity. It's just the nature of the beast. A seemingly innocent post about a sales rep who did a poor job explaining their position turns into a hundred comments where everyone recalls the one time they, too, had poor customer service... four years ago! Not helpful.

I hit "Delete Post" and never look back. It's my page, and my rule is "no negativity." Now, it's not like we're trying to hide the fact there are issues. In any business, there are issues from time to time. But it's unwise to make those issues a focal point. Deal with them in private. If you need help, ask your sponsor. And then if you still feel the need to post about the situation, post about how awesome your sponsor is and how much you appreciate her or his wisdom and guidance.

> I hit "Delete Post" and never look back. It's my page, and my rule is "no negativity."

The way you represent yourself to your corporate office really matters, too. If you have a problem and need to discuss it with the sales support team or an executive, it is always best to be gracious and kind, even if you feel like you've been wronged. Your goal is to have things work out for the good of all involved and to position yourself in a way that ensures people enjoy working with you. You want to have a great reputation. You definitely don't want to be known as a complainer or a whiner. While you might think nobody knows your name, that could change one day, and you'll want your good reputation to precede you.

You are not only representing yourself, but also your team.

You want everyone associated with you to say, "Oh, my gosh, you are so blessed to be part of her team! She's such a positive person and so easy to work with." When you call customer service, remember you're dealing with a human being who is trying to do the best they can, often in difficult situations. Whether you are dealing with your customers, partners, sponsors, or support team, carry cupcakes and rainbows along for the journey!

Now, sometimes life makes it hard to present your best cupcakes and rainbows self, but if you set your mind to it, you can be uplifting and positive even in the worst of times. I've seen that to be true in my own life as I've walked through very difficult times. For instance, few people knew the extent of our financial struggles years ago because it wasn't something we let drag us down. There were days filled with anxiety about how we'd put groceries on the table, but people around us couldn't tell from our attitudes that we were struggling. In fact, our now-grown children have said they had no idea how bad things were because of the way Brian and I handled ourselves during that difficult season. I don't say that to brag on us at all, only to emphasize that, even in hard times, we can choose to have joy and to handle life's most challenging moments with a "glass half full" attitude. We may not always do that perfectly, but we can try!

> When you are the CEO of your own business, you have to operate as such, and you have to see the bigger picture in all circumstances.

A wonderful example of that is my dear friend, Caroline Smith, who has impressed me as much as anyone ever has in this business. She is truly one of the hardest-working people I've ever known. Caroline was a single mom in a season of complete crisis when she decided to say yes to this business. She had every excuse to have a bad attitude and to say no. She had just lost her father unexpectedly at the age of sixty-six, had gone through the breakup of a nine-year relationship, was working a very stressful eighty-hours-a-week job to provide for herself and her son, had her home flood and be filled with mold, had three surgical procedures within a few months, and had crashed her car. Her life had been completely derailed. But when Caroline listened to what this business could offer her, she decided to jump in and work it like her life depended on it—because it really did!

Within the first few months, Caroline brought in over *twenty* business partners. She wasn't in a cupcakes and rainbows season of life, but she didn't walk around with a "woe is me" attitude. She knew if she did that, it wasn't going to attract business partners. I'm not saying we should be fake all the time and never let anyone see us hurting, but I am saying when you are the CEO of your own business, you have to operate as such, and you have to see the bigger picture in all circumstances.

Caroline put her best foot forward, and because she did, people were attracted to her. Many of the people who were drawn to Caroline at that time became happy product customers, and many joined her in business. She shared the good things about her life in those new relationships. She presented herself with joy and positivity. Have you heard the saying, "fake it 'til you make it? Sometimes you have to *fake* cupcakes and rainbows until you *feel* cupcake-y and rainbow-y. Caroline is living proof of that. Her positive attitude in the hardest of times allowed her to build a business that is now bringing in a multiple six-digit annual income. Caroline was able to retire from her full-time job in just seven months and, to date, she has brought in over one hundred direct business partners.

When I heard Caroline's story and learned of the obstacles she had to overcome, it made my own story seem like a cake walk. How about you? Are you derailed right now? If so, that doesn't mean you're out. You just need to find the strength and do whatever needs to be done to get back on track. Do you need to grab ahold of a cupcake and rainbows attitude and exude joy in the midst of your difficult season? We've all been there, and I promise we're cheering you on. If Caroline can do it, you can too!

Chapter 6

The *No's* and Some Other Stuff

"Your time is limited, so don't waste it living someone else's life. Don't be trapped by dogma—which is living with the results of other people's thinking. Don't let the noise of other's opinions drown out your own inner voice. And most important, have the courage to follow your heart and intuition. They somehow already know what you truly want to become. Everything else is secondary."
Steve Jobs, entrepreneur, co-founder and CEO of Apple, Inc.

"Be your own boss, make your own money, and determine your own destiny."
Judge Harry Pregerson, in honor of his daughter, Dr. Katie Rodan

DEBBI

T he majority of the *no's* I heard early on are now a part of my team. Let me say that up front, because sometimes when you are facing a lot of resistance, it might seem hopeless. It's not! Sometimes it just takes time.

Something that helped me in the beginning was this: I didn't take resistance or rejection personally. It wasn't about *me*; it was about *them*.

I remember thinking if a waitress at a restaurant is serving coffee and asks me if I want some, I can say no. My response isn't about her, and it won't hurt her feelings. It's not even about the coffee. I'm just not ready for coffee at the moment. If I never end up getting more coffee, it's still not about her—I'm just missing out on the coffee. Or maybe, just a few moments later, I'll decide I want some coffee after all. Circumstances change, and sometimes they change quickly. My point is, there are many reasons for not having coffee now or not having it at all, but *it's not about the waitress*. She's just offering it to me.

Now, if the waitress isn't friendly, or if she has body odor or something like that, then I'll try my best to not need anything from her! We always want to represent ourselves and our brand to the best of our ability, of course. But assuming nothing is wrong with us or our presentation, we have no reason to feel hurt, depressed, or rejected when someone doesn't take us up on our offer. We are responsible for doing our part by offering the product or position, and the rest is up to the person.

In general, it's often just an issue of timing for people—whether they will join you *now* or *later*. Remember, we don't always know what's going on in their lives. Maybe they are having a health or personal issue that is private, and they *want* to join you, but they can't while they are dealing with that issue. Or maybe financially they are very tight and can't spend a penny right now (which is all the more reason to start, but sometimes they can't see that far yet). Just take their *no* as a *not now*, then follow up later.

Follow up is key! I teach my team to follow back around with everyone until the person asks you to stop. So far, I haven't had a single person ask me to stop. I've also never been obnoxious or aggressive, so keep that in mind. You don't want to be so forceful with someone that it turns the person off (unless it's your sister...right, Wendi?). But there is nothing wrong with saying, "Hey, I know we talked about this before, but right now we have this new [fill in the blank], and I wanted to tell you more about it!." Or, "I know you have been thinking about starting, and right now we have [fill in the blank], so I'm checking back with you to see if this is a better time."

There are many ways to follow up with people without being overbearing, and the person might be excited and grateful you thought to ask again. I've had people wait a month, a year, or even four years to finally say to me, "Yes, Debbi, *now* I am ready, *and* I am *so* excited!" And they had told me no before! We just have to trust they will say yes when the timing is right and they are ready.

> It's often just an issue of timing for people—whether they will join you *now* or *later*.

Also, keep in mind that sometimes a *no* is actually saving you from something you don't need. I truly believe I've had a few *no's* that, looking back, were a blessing in disguise. Some people just don't mesh well, and that's okay.

A very important key in this process is to *listen*. I've found many people do not listen. They don't even hear what people are saying because they are just waiting to speak again. We need to listen and we need to care. When we listen, we hear people's heart and discover where they are. When we listen, we discover how we can help them. But if we don't listen, we only know what we already know. Listen to people! When you genuinely care about them and their needs, they can tell. They need to know the conversation isn't about what you can *get from them*, but what you can *do for them*.

I was in Southern California with Wendi a few years ago, helping her launch her business. We held a few events and organized a couple of meetings. One of those meetings involved a hairdresser friend of hers who wanted to do the business, but she needed the owner of her salon to give her permission to set up a display and discuss the products at work. She was also hopeful he would join the business, which would be a win-win.

> I knew I couldn't let the opinions of others stand in the way of building a business that could change my family's future.

The salon owner said he needed to hear more about it, so we met with him for over an hour, telling him all the smart reasons for her (and him) to do this. It just made sense, so I was certain he would agree. After talking and answering all of his questions, he looked at us and said, "No."

I was shocked. I looked at Wendi. She looked at me. Her friend looked at us. We didn't know what to do. We tried for a good fifteen more minutes to explain why he needed to let her do this, but he just kept saying no.

Finally we drove off in our convertible rental car, a bit stunned. About a mile down the road, Wendi and I looked at each other, and without saying anything, we both burst out laughing. "What were we doing?" We asked each other. "Why did we try so hard to convince him he needed to do this?"

It was a great learning experience. We decided right then and there neither of us would ever try to *convince* someone to say yes. Even if *we* can see this would be amazing for them, and even if *we* want it for them, we cannot want it more then *they* want it. *They have to want it for themselves.* "No" isn't a bad word. Just carry on!

WENDI

If the *no's* have been getting to you, it's time to shake it off and remember, like Debbi said, it's not personal. Many people who have told me no have come back around later and said yes, like Gina. Some haven't said yes, and they still might. If you let those no's affect you to the point where you want to quit, then you'll never win. You have to press on and keep talking until you've talked to hundreds—heck, thousands—of people.

Besides the no's, what are some other things that might be getting in the way of your success? Here are four stumbling blocks that can cause you to fail if you don't overcome them. Together, they spell out the acrostic F.A.I.L.

1. Fear

Fear is a major stumbling block to success. Are you so afraid of what people will think of you that you don't post on social media or send out messages? Do you care more about what people think of you than about your own success? I'm sure you've heard this talked about a lot, but it's imperative we overcome this hurdle.

We all deal with fear at varying levels. Of course I wondered what people would say when I made that first post and sent them that first message. But I didn't let the fear of the unknown paralyze me. I knew I couldn't let the opinions of others stand in the way of building a business that could change my family's future. What good would that do me?

I heard a friend of mine, Gabe Sedlak, say something once that really stuck with me. Gabe is a very successful entrepreneur in direct selling, and when I first started, he said, "If someone's opinion has the power to take you off course, make sure they are paying your bills ten years from today, because they just stole your future." I decided from the very beginning I would not let the opinions of others sway me. Fear has no place here. You have to decide to conquer it.

I shared Gina's story with you earlier. When I asked Gina specifically how she conquered the fears she faced at the beginning of her journey, she shared the following with me.

> In my first three months, I was so worried about what people would think! I was scared they would say no! I was worried they would think, *Why is she doing that?* I did not want to have a launch. I did not want to post on Facebook. I did not want to message people. I did not want to use three-way calls. I should have at least listened in on the free training calls that were offered and read the files on the team pages, but I didn't! I truly thought that just talking to a select few people would yield success, and they would do this with me. But they didn't want to, and I almost quit. Twice.
>
> Then Wendi asked me what I wanted out of my business. I said, "I want what you have, but it's not working for me. I am too busy. I don't have your network. My friends are too busy."
>
> Then she said, "If you want change, you have to change." She said I had a roadmap to success but I wasn't following it. She told me she sacrificed *a lot* to get what she had. She got out of her comfort zone. It was up to me to decide how much I wanted change. *Bam.* I knew she was right.

I dropped my pride that day and said, "Tell me what to do." And I did it. I scheduled my launch. I started posting on Facebook. I started training. I started reading the files. I utilized her for three-way calls. I said goodbye to fear, and everything changed.

Now, get this: after just two years in business, Gina was able to leave her full-time, stressful job. Now she's making an incredible five-digit monthly income and living her life with time and financial freedom.

> You'll never know what greatness lies in front of you if you never take that first step.

What will your story be? Are you letting fear keep you from doing the things you see other successful people doing? I see so many new consultants enroll and then never do a single thing. It's a matter of choice. You have to decide to put one foot in front of the other. Don't let fear defeat you. You'll never know what greatness lies in front of you if you never take that first step.

2. Attitude

Your attitude plays such an important role in your success—or your lack of success. We've already talked a bit about negativity, but let's tie it to how you're branding yourself. If your Facebook posts are woe-is-me posts, or critical-of-other-people posts, or complaining posts, you will absolutely damage your potential for success. The issue won't be whether this business works or not—it will be you and your persona. If you're consistently negative, you'll create an environment the majority of people won't want to be a part of.

We all go through hard stuff in life, and I'm sure you're facing a few challenges, too. But how do you present yourself? If you are trying to run a business utilizing social media, which you should be, you have to think about everything you post, because that is your *brand*. What are your posts saying about you? Do people want to be associated with your brand?

I do a lot of scrolling through social media because I'm out there trying to like and comment on my team's posts to support them. But there are times when I see a post and I just cringe because it's so uncomfortable to read. I'm not promoting being fake or never letting anyone know you're human and you have bad days every now and then; but you have to put thought into how you present yourself. Don't let your negative emotions write your posts. Remember, you don't have to say everything you are feeling. Process your thoughts and emotions first so you can present them in a healthy way, with a positive perspective…or simply don't present them at all! Some things are meant to be private.

> Inconsistency will kill your business. You have to work at it every single day.

A perfect example of this is my friend Amy Cassidy. Amy is very real with her life posts, but they have an uplifting and positive side to them. There is always a redemption story woven into the "life can be hard" reality. One example of this is a post she made a while back about her and her husband, Joey, going to marriage counseling. She talked about the fact that marriage isn't easy, but it didn't come across as a negative post at all. In fact, it was such an incredible post that it went crazy viral and had over 100,000 shares and over 300,000 likes. Talk about putting a positive spin on life! People want to do business with her because her attitude is infectious. Her enthusiasm for life draws people *to* her, instead of a negativity that pushes people *away*. It's no surprise Amy has a thriving team of thousands, is driving her free car, and is at the top tier of our company.

It's not just your attitude that is important but how people *perceive* your attitude. Ask a trusted friend to give you an honest answer to the question, "What does my attitude say about me?" You might think you are a positive person, but if your words and posts reflect negativity, complaining, bitterness, and criticism, people's perspectives of you might not match yours. It's worth thinking about.

Here's another brave question, this one for you to ask yourself. Do you want people just like *you* to join you in business? If the answer to that is no, then it's time to take some steps to change things about yourself and your attitude. Find someone you can be accountable to in this area and improve how you present yourself.

This might be hard to hear, but if you recognize you've been tripped up by this negative-talk stumbling block, you might have to find your business partners outside of your everyday circle. It could be that your reputation has become an obstacle. That's hard to overcome, but it is doable. I'm being honest here, because that's how you grow. Even if you once were a Negative Nelly, if you want it bad enough, you can make it happen. Find new contacts. Work extra hard to recruit, and as your circle of friends and family sees you start to build this business from the ground up—with your new, positive attitude oozing enthusiasm—they will be drawn to you, too. It's just a matter of time. Are you willing to give the time and commitment it requires? You have to decide that!

3. Inconsistency

This one drives me crazy! I can't tell you how many times people have told me they are starting fresh, ready to work hard and get their business going, ready to do everything they've been coached to do. But then...they don't. Or, maybe they do it for a few days or even a few weeks, but then...they don't. And a year later, we have the same conversation. I've seen this cycle way too many times, and it's why I know, that I know, that I know: *inconsistency will kill your business.*

You have to work your business every single day. This is just more honest talk. People tell me they're so bummed their business isn't growing, so I look at their social media pages, and they haven't posted about their business in a week or more. I don't understand that. I mean, of course this is your business, and of course you get to do what you want. But how can you complain about it not working if you're leaving out a key piece of the success puzzle?

The same is true for events. Ask the most successful leaders in our business what they're doing to grow, and they'll tell you they are hosting events. I'm not talking about just one event every now and then. I'm talking about multiple events each month. I did an average of eight events per month my first year in business and an average of six per month my second year. And yes, you might be working full-time while you're building your business, but you can do it! I was working part-time and raising five kids, three of whom were newly adopted from another country—it wasn't like I was sitting around eating bonbons!

My experience is not unique, either. Plenty of our most successful consultants achieved their success while working full-time jobs and raising kids. We have single moms with full-time employment who are succeeding in this business. We have full-time doctors, lawyers, teachers, nurses, pilots. You name it, we've got it. Where there is a will, there is a way. These successful consultants are hosting frequent events; and though it's a sacrifice, the hard work now is worth it to have the time freedom later.

If you're serious about growing your business, I recommend at least two events per month—and that's the minimum. Do this for two to three years. And by the way, I'm talking about you stepping up and taking ownership of your team, not just attending a larger team event someone else organized. *You* put the event together, *you* speak at the event, *you* lead your team. Do that consistently for two years, and then see where you are in your business.

I know what it's like to do events when you're first starting out. You invite a hundred people, and one or two show up, or maybe nobody shows up. Early on in my business, I planned this great event at a really nice clubhouse in my town. My only other local teammate at the time was my sweet friend, Beth, and she made these awesome gift baskets to use for giveaways. But almost nobody came. We were shocked!

But the next Saturday, I was sitting at the coffee shop where I hosted my weekly events, hoping someone would show up. I did that every Saturday for months. Slowly but surely, this team grew: one consultant at a time.

Then I co-hosted events for those new consultants. If someone joined me from out of state, I Skyped in for their first event. Yes, it was a balancing act, and it wasn't always easy. But I did it. And I'm so glad I did! You will be too. Your consistency in this business with the four simple things we keep reminding you to do—posting, hosting, messaging/conversations, and training—*will* pay off in the end. Remember, simple doesn't always mean easy! But none of this is complicated or impossible. Just #DoYourStuff.

4. Lack of vision

What do you believe about yourself and your likelihood of success? What have you done to reinforce your belief system? Do you have a vision board you look at regularly to remind yourself of why you're pushing to reach your goals? Do you have an accountability partner who helps you do what it takes to reach your goals?

Shortly after I started working, I got a white board and set it up in my room so I could see it right when I opened my eyes every morning. I listed each of my direct consultants on that board, and every morning, I prayed for them to be successful. I wrote their current titles and goals beside their names. I tried so hard to be there for them in their first thirty to sixty days to get them off to a strong start: answering their questions, hosting their first couple of events, and doing three-way calls with them. But at some point, the umbilical cord has to be cut. Your desire for them to succeed can't be greater than their own desire to succeed. They have to choose to sink or swim, to believe or give up.

To be honest, many of the 150 people I've personally recruited have decided to quit. Please hear that—*many people have quit*. It happens to all of us. I don't tell you that to discourage you, but to forewarn you. Not everyone wants to work hard for success. In fact, the majority don't.

Here's my point, though: you can't let someone else's lack of vision steal yours. That was something I did right. I decided I would not let someone else's decision affect my vision. I knew I could be successful, with or without them. Can you imagine if I would have quit just because some people I enrolled quit? I would have missed out on everything I have today!

We'll address this in a later chapter, but let me just say the way you succeed in this business is to *recruit*. This is a numbers game, and you can figure only about a third of the people you recruit will really work this business. Don't let the emotional ups and downs of people quitting limit your vision. Keep believing and keep recruiting.

Decide today you won't FAIL. Don't fear, have a great attitude, be consistent, and see the vision!

Chapter 7

Do You Know RITA?

"The most powerful leadership tool you have is
your own personal example."
John Wooden, basketball coach, author, and speaker

DEBBI

I'd never heard the acrostic RITA until one of our business partners, Jamie Walker, used it in a team training. It stands for Recruiting Is The Answer—and it is so true. RITA needs to be your best friend in this business! No doubt about it.

It's not uncommon (okay, it's very common) to bring in business partners and then have them go missing in action. The MIA consultant is someone you become familiar with early on in this business model. That's why it is so important to continually be bringing in new teammates.

I learned early on you can't force someone to work. The old saying, "You can lead a horse to water, but you can't make him drink" is absolutely true. In order to continue to have success, you must find people who *want* to work. Thus, recruiting has to be your top priority.

To tell you the truth, we don't love the term *recruiting*. We'd rather call it *sharing a gift* or *planting seeds* because that's really what you're doing. You are sharing a gift with someone: a new venture that could change their life.

How do you share this business opportunity with someone else? That seems to be the question we get asked the most. It's simple. *You talk.* Seriously. You make conversation with people, and then you let the conversation lead toward the opportunity you want to share with them.

We all talk to people every day. Most the time it is with people we know, whether at work, at our kids' school, in the grocery store, or in our neighborhood. When you know people, you are naturally going to have conversations with them. The real question isn't how to *start* talking to people, but rather how to *turn* the conversation from the weather to "I'd like to tell you about this business..."

There's good news. It's *easy*. If what you have is worth sharing, then it's worth taking a chance, worth getting out of your comfort zone, and worth being told no a few times so you can find the people who will say yes. Once you decide it's worth it, sharing becomes much easier. If you are *confident* and *excited* and truly *believe* in what you're offering, talking about it is natural. You will *want* to talk about it. And then it's up to them to decide. They may need to sleep on it or do their own research first, but your role is to get it out there, to plant the seed. Maybe the seed will grow and produce fruit, and maybe not. But if you never talk to anyone, you'll never know.

> It's worth being told no a few times so you can find the people who will say yes.

If you need a way to start the conversation, just say something sincere and complimentary about the person. "Hi! I love your sweater (shirt, purse, hair…)." She will respond, and now you have something to go from. No matter what the reply is, you can keep the exchange going. Here's a sample conversation:

You: I love your sweater!
Her: Oh, thank you so much.
You: Did you buy it somewhere around here?
Her: Yes, over at Betty's Boutique.
You: I love that store! I used to not be able to shop for myself very often, but now, because of the income I have by owning my own business, I get to treat myself a little more often.
Her: That must be nice, because I love to shop.
You: Well, here, I'd love to give you my business card and get your contact information so I can tell you about my company, because I know you'd love it as much as I do.
Her: I don't have any business cards.
You: That's ok, I'll just write down your email address and send you a little information.
Her: Ok, great. [She gives you her email address and you write it down in the little notebook you carry all the time, or you take a note on your phone.]
You: I just know you'd be great on my team! I can't wait to talk to you in detail about everything. It was so nice to meet you. Have an awesome day!

Voila! You've done it. Now you have the person's contact information, and you can send her follow-up information right away.

What are some keys to having seed-planting conversations with complete strangers on an airplane, at jury duty, or at the furniture store (all of which we have done...and recruited)? Here are a few of them, and Wendi and I are going to tag-team commenting on each one.

1. Have confidence in the opportunity you are presenting

Every time you speak with someone, you need to be confident in what you are sharing. Remember, your story is your story, and no one can argue with that. If you have seen your products work, if you have seen this business help you, then you can speak with confidence. You aren't trying to manipulate people or deceive them! You are sharing a gift, something that could change their lives.

I travel several times a year doing speaking engagements and events. A lot of those times, I travel alone while Steve stays home with our boys. When I am traveling solo, I get a little giddy, because I can't wait to see whom I will sit by on the plane. I know I will find a way to talk to them about this business opportunity.

My first year in the business, I sat on a plane next to a guy who had his little boy with him, a really cute, sweet kid. I told the dad, "Your little boy is adorable." That genuine compliment started a conversation.

He asked me, "Do you have kids?" We talked back and forth about life, family, where we lived, and more. Then he asked me, "Where are you going?"

I was actually headed to a business retreat, so I told him about that, which led to him asking me questions about my business. By the time the plane landed, the guy could not wait to have his wife (who was seated toward the back of the plane with their daughter) talk to me about my business. He said she loved skincare, and he saw a great opportunity. She signed up a couple of days later over the phone, all because of a conversation on a plane.

Another time, I had jury duty. I literally prayed I would be able to share my business that week with someone who *needed* it. It's a *gift*, as I said, and I truly believe that. On the first day, I overheard a woman talking about being fired from her job after twelve years. She had gone into work like any normal day, and they told her they had dissolved her position. She was given no warning and no reason. I heard her say she needed something to do from home because her severance was almost gone, and she really wanted to be home with her kids now.

I knew I needed to talk to her because I had something that could be perfect for her. I never want to be obnoxious or make anyone feel awkward, so I kept waiting for an opportunity to speak to her naturally. If all else failed, I figured I would tell her I loved her shoes or bag or something else I truly liked. All week, I tried to find a way to talk to her without success.

On the last day of jury duty, she was talking to a couple of people about a situation that happened in my city many years before. I knew the story, and I knew the people she was talking about. *Open door!* I chimed in, "Oh! I know them! Hi, my name is Debbi." And we began a natural conversation.

Before leaving, I told her I had overheard her say she needed a job. I told her I had an opportunity that had changed my life, something I was able to do from home. I said I'd like to share it with her, and she was interested. I pulled out my phone, went to Facebook, asked for her name, found her on Facebook, and sent her a friend request as we stood there. She took out her phone and accepted my request right then.

I was going to wait until the following week to reach out to her so I didn't seem too anxious, but before I could contact her, she reached out to me. She said, "I can't stop thinking about what you told me. I'd like to hear more." She soon joined my team.

I shared a *gift* with her, and she accepted it. It was just what she needed. What if I hadn't been bold enough to share with a stranger? I would have robbed her of something wonderful. When you look at what you have as a gift you are offering, it changes everything.

WENDI

I couldn't agree more with Debbi about the importance of being bold and having confidence in the opportunity you are presenting. Once I started making good money with my company, there were some things we were pretty desperate to purchase, and one of those was a new bed. We decided to go to a really nice mattress store and get a high-quality bed.

Of course as I was talking to the sales guy, I made a point to tell him it was my new job that had allowed us to be able to afford a mattress like that. And of course he asked me what I did (because that is how a natural conversation flows). I was then able to tell him all about the business. I already had his contact information because I had just made a purchase from him and had his business card in hand, but I gave him my business card and included a sample of one of our products, and I asked him to share it with his wife. I told him I'd call to follow up in a couple days to see what they thought of the product. But just like Debbi's story, before I called him back, he called me to set up a follow-up meeting, and soon his wife joined my team. If I had never said anything, his wife wouldn't have joined me, and we would have all missed out on the benefits.

DEBBI

---

2. Use social media

You probably have many contacts on Facebook alone, plus Instagram, Twitter, or any other social media platforms where you have a presence. Besides that, how many names are in your phone address book? How about email addresses? Those are *contacts*. Those are *prospects*. Use them!

Reach out, one by one, and send a personalized message to every person you know. You are simply planting seeds. Some will respond. Some won't. Some will join right away. Some will wait a year. That's okay! Time is your friend as you grow your team. As long as you are doing daily activity, you will grow, seed by seed, step by step.

> Time is your friend as you grow your team.

WENDI

When I first started, Debbi told me to set a goal to message one hundred people, so that's what I did. Since then, I've looked back at some of my original messages, and one thing I notice is they were often too long and detailed. Don't feel like you need to tell someone everything about your company the first time you reach out. Just say something like, "Hey Sally, it's so great to follow your journey here on Facebook. You may have seen that I've become a consultant with [business name]. I am so excited about this company and their products, and I would love to have an opportunity to tell you a little bit about it. Could you jump on the phone with me maybe Thursday night at eight or Friday morning at ten?" In my experience, these shorter, to-the-point messages are much better at getting a response from the recipients.

> They will keep watching you, and often it's just a matter of time.

You can also attach what is called an "opportunity call" or "opportunity video" along with your message. I include a link to one of these in every single initial message I send out. These are audio or video recordings that tell the story of how other consultants achieved success. When including one, try to find a story that will resonate with the person you're sending the call or video to. For instance, if you're reaching out to a realtor, find a success story from another realtor. If your prospect is a teacher, send a teacher story. If he or she is a doctor, send a doctor story.

You can also use opportunity calls as an excuse to reach back out to someone you contacted earlier. "Hey, I came across this story and it made me think of you. I'd love for you to listen to it (or watch it) if you'd like! Then let's chat so I can answer any questions you have. How does Thursday night at eight o'clock sound for a quick call?"

Another great thing to include in your message is an invitation to an event you're hosting. Of course, you have to have events on the calendar in order to do this (and as we've said, you should definitely have multiple events planned each month).

DEBBI

---

3. Be patient

This is just *truth*. You cannot expect everyone to jump in, and honestly, most people take a little time. As I said before, many people have told me "no" or "maybe later" or even flat-out ignored me, only to end up joining me a month later or a year later. Some have even joined four years after I first reached out to them! Be patient. They will keep watching you, and often it's just a matter of time.

Sometimes people want to wait for a while to see if it's real. That is totally understandable. Many people have been burned. *Show* them you are real by being *consistent* and *persistent*. Those are keys to your success. Don't be hot and cold, on and off, yes and no. When you say you are going to do something, do it, and do it *all the way*. People will respect that. They *are* watching you.

Statistically speaking, I've heard people have to see something eight times before they act on it in some way. Keep going! You have a commercial to air. How many times are people seeing it?

WENDI

One of my besties, Amy, is someone I had to be really patient with. I *knew* she would be amazing in this business, so I stayed patient and persistent. Shortly after I enrolled, I sent Amy a brief message telling her I knew she was happy in her job as a nurse practitioner, but I would love to tell her about my new business. Amy was very successful, but I did not let fear keep me from talking to her. We were friends. We sang on the worship team at our church together. What's the worst that could have happened? So I sent the note. She sent a nice response to my first email, but it was basically a "Thanks, but no thanks" reply.

About a month later, I reached out a second time and told her all about a new consultant on my team who was also in the medical field. I shared that lady's story so Amy could see she was already having great success. Again, she was nice enough to respond, but she told me she was way too busy.

Two months later, she happened to post on her Facebook page about being exhausted and not getting to spend much time with her kids because of the long shifts she'd been working. I genuinely care about Amy, and I truly believed our company would be a huge blessing to her. I messaged her again and gave her an update on my business and the other woman's business I had previously mentioned to her. In that short time, the other woman was already making a sizable four-digit income.

> People will thank you for not giving up on them and for being brave enough to push through.

Again, Amy was quick to respond, but this time, it was a *strong* no. I mean, it was an absolute. So I did what any fearless recruiter does: I asked her to please send her friends to me so I could tell them about the business and products. She assured me she would.

Three months later, I messaged her to tell her I was going to be in her city, and I straight up asked if she'd host an event for me. Why not? Again, there's just nothing to lose as long as you're being kind and not simply hounding someone. Amy knew I cared about her, and we had a real relationship, so she said she would host the event for me. She's awesome like that.

The next month, she called to tell me she had decided to join me in business because the friends she was inviting to the event were saying yes, and she realized it would be silly for her to build a business for me when she could be building one for herself. Today, Amy is one of our most successful leaders, making an amazing seven-figure annual income!

Can you imagine if I would have let fear keep me from continuing to reach out to Amy? Remember, you have nothing to lose and so much to gain. And people will thank you for not giving up on them and for being brave enough to push through.

4. Have fun and be excited

People want to be part of something *fun*. Life can be hard, and people want to participate in something that isn't heavy or depressing. Is your team exciting and fun? Let people wonder what you are doing! Make them curious. Show them, whether on social media or in conversations, that not only is money being made in your business, but friendships are being developed on your team.

Camaraderie is a huge part of life. Debbi and I have made some of our dearest friends through this business. People want to feel like they belong, they want to be appreciated, and they want to be built up. Is your team something others would want to join? When you enjoy *what* you do and *who* you do it with, you will find people will be attracted to you like never before.

DEBBI

Wendi is exactly right! I've always told my team to make things fun. People want to be part of something *good*. They want to work alongside great people who enjoy what they do. They aren't going to join someone who is apathetic, monotone, and boring. Our team meetings, if you can even call them that, are not your typical boring, PowerPoint meetings. We have fun, we tell stories, and we share—real people to real people.

We also need to remember people are watching us even when we are not in "work mode." Actually, you could say we are working (or "on call") all the time because we are always around people. Our enthusiasm motivates us to share what we are excited about even when we aren't trying to. For example, in my second year of business, Steve and I were in Hawaii on a trip I had earned. There was a group of us there, and we were having a wonderful time hanging out, laughing, and simply enjoying a welcome reward for our work. One day I was lying on a lounge chair by the pool, talking to a couple I had just met there. Eventually casual conversation led to me telling them who we were and why we were there. They were very interested in hearing more, and we had a great talk.

Meanwhile, Steve was talking to some guys by the bar area. I had finished my conversation with the couple and had just closed my eyes when Steve came over and said, "Hey, Debbi, I want you to meet Bettina Kelley." I sat up and saw a cute young woman who, judging by her uniform, worked at the resort. After introducing us, Steve told me he had ordered a drink from Bettina, and they started talking about our trip. She had seen our group and noticed what a great time we were having. That had sparked her interest, so Steve said, "Let's go over and talk to my wife, and she can tell you more about it."

Bettina and I chatted for a few minutes, but because of her wonderful integrity, she asked if we could meet the next day, since she was on the clock and wanted to be respectful of her job. I loved that about her! We made plans to meet the next day at a nearby restau-

> I love sharing stories because they resonate with people. Facts tell, but stories sell,

rant. When we met again, I shared the business opportunity and told her about the awesome products we have, about our team, and about what this business had done for so many. I love sharing the stories because they resonate with people. "Facts tell, but stories sell," says the old sales adage.

Bettina was so excited to get started that she became a consultant on the spot. To this day she is an active, growing business owner on my team. I've watched her flourish, and I must say, she enjoys life! Being in business for herself has given her extra freedom to spend with her kids, and she can work anytime, anywhere, and any way she wants.

Steve and I were just doing what we do every day. We are excited to share with others, and we love seeing how their lives can be changed and even blessed. Not only does enthusiasm make work not feel like work, but it's contagious, attractive, and almost irresistible.

Chapter 8

Unicorns vs. Llamas

"If your actions create a legacy that inspires others to dream more, learn more, do more, and become more, then you are an excellent leader."
Dolly Parton, singer, songwriter, producer, actress, author, and businesswoman

DEBBI

A t one of our business conventions a while back, a woman came up to me and said, "Oh my gosh, it's *you*! You *are* real! I thought maybe you were just a unicorn!" I thought it was cute, and we both laughed. Then it happened again, on a different occasion. And later on, someone said it on my team page. The title caught on, and to this day, my team calls me a unicorn.

I actually love the title, because I'm a Disneyland girl. I grew up in Southern California, so Disneyland is a feel-good place for me. I always wanted to be Alice in Wonderland. To this day, anytime I am in California visiting Wendi, I go to Disneyland. Who isn't completely happy there? I love wonder and fantasy. I'm the cupcakes and rainbows person, so it makes sense that I love unicorns, too.

I know some people think I am too flowery. I had someone say that to my face once. I remember thinking, *Too flowery? What does that even mean?* Maybe she thought I lived in La La Land because I don't talk about negative things. It's not that I ignore reality—I just don't dwell on the bad things, and I quickly find a way to see something good in most anything, if it's possible. In life, there are tough things. Too many of them! If I can find a way to have more laughter, peace, and kindness, to extend a smile and thoughtfulness to others more often, why wouldn't I do that? That's who I am and how I live.

Here's my point, though: not everyone is alike. You aren't me, and I'm not you. Maybe you aren't a unicorn. Maybe you've never been told you're flowery. *That's okay!* But that doesn't mean you can't do what I've done. The idea behind the whole "unicorns and llamas" thing (Wendi will explain the llama title later) is simply that everyone is different. Even Wendi and I— sisters with the same background and similar values—are actually very different.

For example Wendi talks a lot more than me (and a lot louder!). Have you noticed her portions in this book are longer than mine? I rest my case! Honestly, though, I am perfectly happy letting her do the bulk of the talking when we are together. Also Wendi loves the stage, whereas I could take it or leave it. When I was younger, I used to dread speaking in public. Now I've gotten to where I am comfortable onstage, and I even enjoy myself. But when I speak at large events, it takes me a day or two to bounce back because it exhausts me. Not Wendi! She's ready to go the next day. She thrives in that environment. We are different, but we are both succeeding in business.

I've had many people say to me, "Debbi, I just can't do this! I'm not like you!" I tell them (gently, of course) that is an excuse. People of all personality types can be successful—introvert, extrovert, or ambivert. I hardly even know what I am. I used to be an introvert, but I've been told I am an ambivert now, which apparently means I am a mix of both. All I know is, I love being home, and I love having my pajamas on by five o'clock in the evening. But when I am out doing my thing, I love that, too! People from all backgrounds can be successful—doctors, lawyers, teachers, actors, pastors, hairstylists, college students, grandmas, men, women...I could go on and on. All are different. All are unique. There is no "ideal" type of person. If one can do it, then another can do it.

Different isn't just okay—it's better, because we can learn from one another. I've learned so much watching Wendi grow her business and team. She has done more in this business in such a short time than anyone has. She says all the time she grew her business by just doing what I do, but along the way, she started doing things within her team I had not done, and I learned from her.

> Different isn't just okay—it's better.

There is a lot to be said about her style, what she does, and how she does it. Being different is good. You don't want to be just like me or just like Wendi. Be you! And be the best *you* that you can be. You don't have to be a unicorn or a llama. Be a koala!

One of my business partners, Darci Schmidt, is very different from me, yet she is experiencing incredible success. Way back in our high school years, Darci went to school with Steve. I attended another school, but I remember being at Steve's football games and seeing Darci on the drill team and thinking she was so pretty and friendly. When I started doing this business, Darci came to my mind. I never really knew her well, but through the years, I had heard she was very successful in her corporate career. She and Steve were friends on Facebook (social media is an incredible tool—have you noticed?), so I sent her a friend request. I figured if she was friends with Steve on Facebook, she wouldn't mind being friends with me. She accepted the request.

A few weeks passed, and one day she sent me a message. I had intended to send *her* a message, but I wanted to wait a while and let a relationship develop naturally. Otherwise it might seem I had only sent the friend request to tell her about my business. Because of the effectiveness of social media, though, she had already seen my page and noticed what I was doing. She took the initiative to inquire about it. I'm telling you, leverage social media! Don't worry that people might judge you for sharing a product you love. Who really cares what they think? Remember Gabe Sedlak's words: "Those people aren't paying your bills!"

> Pray about it. Laugh about it. And go find a rainbow!

I answered Darci's questions, and sure enough, she joined me. She told me she knew a good thing when she saw it, and she didn't want to miss this chance. Today Darci leads a team of thousands. She surpassed the six-figure annual income she was receiving from her corporate job and was able to retire. Darci has also become one of my dearest friends, which is yet another blessing from this business. I'll never forget the day she called me and said, "You saved my life!" This truly is a life-changing opportunity.

My point is, Darci and I are very, very different. She has a college degree, Master of Science in Management. I don't. She didn't have kids at the time (although she does now). I have five. She was a highly successful leader in the corporate world, a total career person who had won awards in her field. Not me—not even close! Yet we can both do this business. She didn't need to be just like me, and I don't need to be just like her. This business is an equalizer, and I love that. If you are determined, you can do it.

Don't just tolerate differences—learn to *enjoy* them. As a leader, you will have people on your team who don't see eye to eye with you about everything. That's okay! Learn to accept other viewpoints and even to learn from them. Leadership, by definition, means you'll have multiple people following you. And multiple people mean multiple ideas, opinions, personalities, strengths, and weaknesses. It's a team of people, not clones, and your differences are what make you stronger as a team. Don't get frustrated with yourself because you aren't just like someone else, and don't get frustrated with your team because they aren't just like you.

Here's a leadership tip that is often underrated but is one of my absolute favorites: *learn to laugh.* Wendi and I laugh a lot, often at each other. For example, I am very technically challenged, but Wendi is quick to figure stuff out. I have to Google everything, and I still don't get it right. Just while writing this book, I am sure Wendi and our editor, Justin, wanted to toss their computers off their desks because I couldn't figure out how to share files or sync files or whatever it is—I don't even know what it's called, much less how to do it. But instead, Wendi just laughs (either *with* me or *at* me, I'm not sure which). That's so much better than getting angry. Then together, we figure things out.

Our differences make life exciting and colorful. I challenge you, let go of things you can't control, and be okay with those who are different than you. You be you. Let them be them. Pray about it. Laugh about it. And go find a rainbow!

WENDI

Well, Debbi said I talk and write more than her, but I'd like to point out her part of this chapter is *long*! Who's the chatty one now? All kidding aside, Debbi is a very rare person. She possesses a set of qualities that make her different, valuable, and effective. She has worked hard to be a unicorn in this business, and she deserves the title. I had someone call me a unicorn once, but I just looked at her and said, "Debbi's the unicorn, so I'll have to be something else." I didn't want to horn in on Debbi's whole unicorn thing!

Debbi pushes the rainbows and cupcakes thing pretty hard (go, Debbi, go!), so at one of our company's conventions, she asked everyone to wear a rainbow ribbon so they could easily be identified as part of her team. I found a pin that was a unicorn with a rainbow mane—total jackpot! I put that thing on my lanyard and wore it with pride. But the second day, I looked down and saw the horn of the unicorn had fallen off. There I was, stuck with a hornless unicorn pin. That's when it hit me. *That looks like a llama... hey, I'll be a llama*! I love llamas. Llamas are very social animals, and they're very smart. I would make a great llama! My very fashionable niece, Cassidi, told me llamas are the new unicorns. Debbi even bought me the cutest pair of tennis shoes with llamas on them. Truly a fashion statement. I am hip and cool.

From the day the unicorn's horn fell off to this, I see Debbi as a unicorn and me as a llama. Debbi and I are similar, but we're different. Debbi has the horn (because she's bossy and all) and I have soft fur and am pleasant to be around. I'm kidding! Anyway, the point of this story is that we are different, and that's great. You don't need to be just like other people. You are *you*. They are *them*. Debbi covered that in detail above.

But regardless of your personality, background, or style, you do need to be a *good leader* if you expect people to follow what you're doing. So what does that look like? How can you lead your team toward success?

I read a great quote by Andy Stanley awhile back, and I have often repeated it when doing leadership training: "Leaders instill courage in the hearts of those who follow. This rarely happens through words alone. It generally requires action...Somebody has to go first."

In other words, if you want to be successful, you have to do tangible, visible actions so people have something to follow. When you set goals and then step up and reach those goals, you show people the way. You have to lead by your actions, and your team naturally duplicates that. We can talk until we're blue in the face about all we're going to do, but if we don't actually do it, it won't do any good. No one will move, because they are following the leader... and she's standing still.

Doing actions to *teach* people is one thing, but doing things *for* other people is another. If I've done anything right in this business, I think I've done a good job at knowing how to lead people to a place of self-sufficiency. If we are constantly doing everything for people, they will never learn to do things for themselves. I mentioned earlier it would be way too hard to cross Niagara Falls on a tightrope while trying to carry people. It's much smarter business to follow the "teach people to fish" concept. I think (and hope!) my direct consultants would say I have done a good teaching them to fish.

I tell people I'm recruiting, "I will help you for the first thirty to sixty days, but then you're on your own, and you will either sink or swim." I literally say that! I'm not being harsh—I'm setting healthy expectations. People need the chance to spread their wings and fly. They need to watch me fly first, but they also need to believe *they* can fly, and ultimately, they need to show *their team* how to fly. If I'm the only one flying, my business will never get off the ground.

When I'm training newbies, we talk about all that upfront. I explain how they can call or text me to get answers to their questions. In the beginning, if a newbie asks me a question, I'll immediately give the answer. The second time the person asks a question along the same lines, I might say something like, "Remember what we talked about last time, you can find that answer in such and such place," and then I'll give the answer. But the third time the newbie asks a similar question, I give some space to allow the person to think about it. More often than not, I'll get a "never mind, found it" follow-up text within a short time.

> Lazy doesn't have a place in leadership.

When people are made to think for themselves, it's very likely they will. Sometimes people are just being lazy, and asking you is the easier way. Don't be that person yourself, and don't enable that behavior in others. A strong leader will do her best to find the answers on her own, especially if she's already been told where those answers can easily be found. Lazy doesn't have a place in leadership.

Unfortunately, some people never received help from the sponsor who brought them into the business. Nobody took the time to teach them how to fish. That is sad, and it does happen; however, I've also seen people succeed without a helpful sponsor. It depends primarily on the attitude and work ethic of the person. I have close friends who have reached the highest levels in our company with almost no help from their sponsor. If anything, their sponsor actually made things more difficult for them. But they made the choice to overcome, and they not only succeeded, they excelled. How? They figured out how to fish on their own. They utilized upline, power partners, corporate training, Google, whatever it took. They made a choice to become the leader who was missing in their journey. Now, they are leading teams of multiple thousands and have learned balanced leadership.

Another thing: continue to fish while you're teaching other people to fish. You have to keep recruiting and building your own business while leading your team. I see too many people quit fishing for themselves long before they should. They fished for a while and caught a few fish, but somewhere along the line they decided that was enough. Now they're standing around, baiting hooks and throwing in the line for people they've brought into the business. Eventually that gets really hard and time-consuming, so they call in a professional fisherman to come talk about fishing. Pretty soon everyone is standing around listening to him talk about fishing, and they've *all* stopped fishing. Plus, the "professional" charged everyone for a ticket, so now the fishermen don't have as much money left to purchase the necessities they need to continue to fish!

The original fisherman would have been much better off continuing to fish and letting his new recruits *see* him fishing and *see* him enjoying the results of his catch. Many people have stopped fishing way too early, and now they're wondering why they're still hungry. I believe each person should continue to recruit until they have a minimum of one hundred people direct to them. And if you find only a third of those are working hard to grow a business, keep fishing for more! Don't stop fishing in order to teach your team how to fish—the best way to teach them to fish is by *fishing*.

Because of the value we place on *doing* the work and not just *talking* about the work, we hold the trainers who lead our weekly team training sessions to the highest standard. We tell our team these consultants have achieved a particular title in the company; therefore, unless the training consultant is maintaining that level of success, he or she is not allowed to train. We believe it's extremely important our team be trained by the best of the best, which means people who are actually *doing* the tasks and *reaping* the rewards from having done them.

There are a lot of people who call themselves trainers and actually do a great job pumping up the adrenaline of the listener, but have they done the work and achieved the success they are training people for? I've noticed that more than ever, there seems to be a certain celebrity trainer mentality going on. People find their flavor-of-the-month trainer, and that person becomes bigger than life. The problem is, people are being guided by someone who, perhaps, hasn't even had great success with what they are training on.

As a trainer, I believe you shouldn't hold your cards closely to your chest, but you should put your credentials out to your audience and make sure they know what level of success you've had. And as a listener, I believe you should do your research and know whom you're taking advice from. I see far too many people spending far too much time listening to "celebrity" trainers (even paying huge sums to bring them in for private trainings) instead of working their business.

I'm not saying there aren't great trainers out there, and I'm not saying there is anything wrong with utilizing them once in a while to encourage your team; but listening to daily trainings or organizing on-going events actually *takes away* from the business you need to be building. And if *you* are doing that, your team will duplicate it, and no one will be working.

Your team is smart enough to go to the bait shop and buy some bait. Your team is smart enough to bait the hook. Your team is smart enough to throw a line. And your team is smart enough to reel in a fish. Let them fish! And if you'll excuse the terrible mixed metaphor, letting them figure out how to fish by watching you fish is also the best way for them to "spread their wings and fly," which I talked about earlier.

As for you, *keep fishing*. Reel in anyone and everyone who wants to fish with you. Reel in some unicorns, some llamas, and even some koalas. (Those mixed metaphors just keep coming!) When you do that, you'll end up with a healthy, successful team where everyone works and everyone enjoys the results of their work.

Chapter 9

Play Nice

"Do to others as you would have them do to you."
Jesus

DEBBI

How do people feel when they've been around you? Do they feel like they've been seen? Do they feel like they've been heard? Do they feel special? Or do they feel like they weren't even noticed or don't even matter? Or worse, do they feel like you're annoyed by them? I never want anyone to feel worse about themselves after they've been with me. On the contrary: I want people to feel *better* than before. I want them to leave feeling happy and loved.

People are precious! I may not agree with everyone about everything, but I still love them. We have to learn to not discount anyone just because we are different. Sure, not everyone is my favorite…but I'm not their favorite, either! We may not vote the same. We may not dress the same. We may not worship the same. That's okay! We can still be nice and respectful. They are still humans, with real souls and real feelings; and everyone deserves to be treated with kindness.

Personally, I take it a step further: I want everyone I meet to feel loved, celebrated, and special. A few years ago, I was at our company's convention in Atlanta. I had just finished speaking at a training session with one of my business partners. Our husbands were with us, and we were walking through the crowded event center. We were stopped every few feet by people in the business who wanted to take a quick picture with us and meet us. Some were from my team, some were not.

It is very humbling, to say the least, when people stop me to tell me I have inspired them in some way or encouraged them in their business or in life. I truly love taking a moment to look at them, listen to them, and give them a hug. (I am a hugger, by the way, as you'll discover for yourself if you and I ever meet in person!) It is precious to me to meet people on my team and in the business I haven't met before.

This particular day, a young lady approached me and introduced herself. I welcomed her and greeted her like I always do. Her name was Natalie Heinrich. She told me she was a fairly new consultant, not a high title in the company, and she was so excited to meet me because she was on my team and was thankful for my training. I hugged her and looked her in the eyes. I took the time to chat with her for a few minutes. She told me about her job as a physician's assistant. I thanked her for her hard work and told her I was so glad she was on my team. Then she took a picture with me, and we said goodbye.

I didn't think too much about it at the time because I meet hundreds of people at conventions. But years later Natalie reminded me about that chance encounter. She told me to this day, she frequently tells the story of our first meeting because it profoundly influenced her life and business. In her own words:

> I will never forget meeting you for the first time at convention. I had just started my business. You didn't know

me from Adam, but you treated me like gold. I will never forget it! The way you made me feel important has stuck with me since that day, and I strive to pay it forward to those I come in contact with. You are a true example of treating everyone the same, no matter who they are or where they come from. This has had a great impact on my business, but more importantly, as a person in general. Love you!

That day, I had no idea how much our quick conversation inspired and empowered her. Natalie says she couldn't believe I would take the time to stop, talk to her, and hug her. To look at her and listen to her. To make her feel *special*. I didn't know her. I didn't know what her success would be, and it didn't matter. Everyone deserves kindness, attention, and celebration.

If we don't use what God has given us to help others, it's all for nothing! I don't mean to be morbid here, but each of us will die one day. That's just the truth. When we are gone, only what we did for others will live on. I want my business to propel me to a place where I can touch more lives. *That* is the legacy I want to leave.

> When we are gone, only what we did for others will live on.

By the way, today, Natalie is one of my good friends! She *soared* to the top of the company, and she has an incredible team that she leads with passion. She is one of my team's top earners, and she was able to retire from her PA career. I am so proud to know her and be her friend.

In your business, on your team, and in life, how do you make people feel, no matter who they are? Do they matter to you, even if they aren't in your top ten? Do you stop, look them in the eyes, and listen to them, even if you've never heard their name before? My awesome assistant, Marny, always says, "Treat people with respect. Period. No matter if they are the person cleaning the toilet or the person who invented the toilet." How profound is that?

> As you grow your business, make other people feel loved and appreciated and valued.

Looking back, it wouldn't have mattered to me if I would have known who Natalie would become. I'd love her the same, just for who she was right then. That is what I did, after all. And she remembers to this day how I made her feel! To me, that is greater success than any level of income or recognition I might have received. *People matter most.*

How do you want to be treated? Have you ever been made to feel less than enough by someone? Has someone ever looked at you as if to say, "You're bothering me"? That's not a good feeling! As you grow your business, make other people feel loved and appreciated and valued. That will *inspire* and *empower* them. Maybe they were never told, "Thank you for your hard work!" You could be the one who gives them something to run toward. People just want to be loved. Go and love well! It will feel great to you and to them, and I believe it will come full circle.

WENDI

One of the best things about this business—and one of the trickiest things about this business—is relationships. This is a relationship business through and through. Due to the nature of our products, the majority of our consultants are women... which means there are a lot of hormones flinging about! And I'm only partly joking.

As a team leader, it's always interesting to navigate feelings and emotions. Debbi and I have both been blessed with teams that overall have very little drama. But some drama is inevitable in any team, and you have to know what you're going to do with that.

The truth is, you may not love working with every single person on your team. That's okay. But like Debbi said above, you *do* have to be loving. You just do! The differences of opinion you encounter along the journey are natural, expected, and even healthy. Decide today you're going to follow this simple, biblical approach: "If it is possible, as far as it depends on you, live at peace with everyone" (Romans 12:18, NIV). That's wisdom!

How can we "play nice" in the face of misunderstandings, miscommunication, or offense? It's not that hard, actually: it just requires wisdom and intentionality. We have to take the time to calm down, think clearly, and ask ourselves how we can love and serve others. Here are a few situations I've seen recently. I suspect you have seen or will see them, too.

1. Someone else recruits someone you've been talking to.

This is a bummer, for sure; but unless someone was truly unethical (in which case, you'd need to discuss the situation with your company's compliance department), you just have to let this go. Sure, you will probably be upset, but do your best to shake it off quickly and move on.

Our company has a code of ethics, and it's really important for each business owner to be familiar with that code. Upon approaching new prospects, you should always ask, "Has anyone ever talked to you about our company or products before?" If their answer is yes, you need to encourage them to circle back to the person who spoke to them first.

Having said that, however, there is a big difference between having a meaningful, back-and-forth conversation with someone versus just sending a quick note letting the person know about the company you represent. I have always said you can't claim prospects. In order for you to "lay claim" to a potential consultant, you need to have had an ongoing conversation with that person. The prospect must have been interested enough to have real discussions with you about the opportunity.

For example, I can send a note to Betty Sue, and Betty Sue can write back and say, "Thanks so much for this information," but that does not make Betty Sue "mine." Later, if Jaymee reaches out to Betty Sue, Betty Sue can buy products and/or join Jaymee in business. There's nothing unethical about that. Disappointing for me, maybe; but it's just a normal occurrence in this business, and it's nothing to get bent out of shape about.

But if Betty Sue and I have talked multiple times, and maybe Betty Sue even went to an event with me, then she is more than just a prospect. She is "my" contact, and other consultants from my company should not try to sign her up. Let's say Jaymee reaches out to Betty Sue after Betty Sue and I have had meaningful, back-and-forth conversation about the business opportunity. Typically, Betty Sue will mention that to Jaymee. Then Jaymee should say, "That's so great you've been talking to Wendi. You need to reach back out to her. She's amazing and you'll love working with her." (Aww, thank you, Jaymee!) You do that because that's what you'd want someone to do for you! That's the Golden Rule, and it's the best way to do business.

If you genuinely feel someone has crossed a line and violated your company's code of ethics (or if someone accuses you of violating it), I usually suggest attempting to work it out one-on-one first. If that doesn't work, though, or if you feel you need help knowing the right course of action, you should certainly reach out to your company's compliance department.

2. You have a sponsor who isn't working the business and isn't helping you.

This is a hard one because everyone who joins the business deserves to have help at the beginning of their journey. In fact, our particular policies and procedures manual states it is the sponsor's obligation to help the newbie get started. Unfortunately, many don't. But I know of *many* consultants who did not receive any help from their sponsors and yet are extremely successful.

One friend of mine, whom I referenced earlier, not only didn't have help from her sponsor, but her sponsor actually made things much more difficult for her. I won't give the details, but it resulted in some really, really hurtful moments for my friend. But guess what? She found her own way. She was determined to succeed, and not even a "less than helpful" sponsor was going to get in her way. She decided to become the type of sponsor she wanted. She found a power partner so she could have some accountability, and she set goals and achieved them. If she can do it, you can, too!

Side note: don't be that type of sponsor! If you've said yes to the business, then please, work your business and help those you've brought in get started working theirs.

3. You have a sponsor or teammate whom you do not see eye to eye with; in fact, you don't really like him or her very much.

It doesn't matter. *Really*. Sure, it would be nice if life were always easy. But "cupcakes and rainbows" doesn't mean life is easy. Rather, it means keeping a good attitude even when circumstances and people are *not* easy to deal with. Often you have to do business with people who aren't your favorites. When you're in this situation, the smartest thing you can do is not say or do anything that would cause your behavior to be in question. Less is more. For instance, don't gossip about that person to other business partners. That doesn't do any good, and it puts other people in an awkward position. Plus you wouldn't want that person doing that to you. Maintain your integrity and don't say anything to anyone you might regret later. It's not worth it.

> "Cupcakes and rainbows" doesn't mean life is easy. It means keeping a good attitude even when circumstances and people are *not* easy.

I've had people call me and try to put me in the middle of their disagreements, and I've told them I won't respond. I just won't. Nothing I could say would help. Why? Because one person would go back to the other and say, "Well, Wendi said *blah blah blah.*" And then the other person would think I've been talking behind his or her back ... and we're back in junior high. I won't do it.

Recently, when something of that sort happened, I responded with a brief and kind message: "I'm so sorry you are having a difficult time and you're hurting. Please know I'm praying this gets resolved quickly. You guys will need to work it out between the two of you. Of course, if there is a compliance issue, please reach out to that department." Done. I won't discuss it again. We are adults. We must act like it.

I was once front and center to quite a disagreement between two consultants. Bottom line, they just rubbed each other the wrong way. Often! When they were in the same room, you could sense the tension. But I watched as those two women decided to have a mature conversation about their issues, and I saw the relationship restored. It was awesome. Today, they work together beautifully and actually enjoy each other's company. If we handle ourselves with class, there's a real chance for relationship restoration.

4. Whatever else you're having issues with.

When you're the CEO of your own business, there will always be issues that arise that you have to handle with grace. You might get frustrated with an executive at corporate, for example. Someone might copy one of your social media posts word for word and present it as their own. A business partner might schedule an event with a panel of speakers but not invite you to speak. Someone you brought into the company might give someone else credit for her success in spite all you did to help her along the way. Someone might promise to do everything you say and work hard to have success but then do absolutely nothing in spite of all your attempts to help.

Some (or all!) of that will probably happen. I'm just being real! And, when it does, you will "win" if you react with grace and with a true desire to see others succeed regardless of how your feelings might have been hurt. In the end, the best thing we can do is think the very best of people, give them the benefit of the doubt, and work hard to be fabulous team players.

Chapter 10

Leave a Legacy

"The bottom line in leadership isn't how far we advance
ourselves but how far we advance others."
*John C. Maxwell, author, speaker, pastor,
and leadership expert*

DEBBI

I f we can do this, you can, too! Listen, don't let anything stop
you. You *can* succeed in this business, but you have to want
it, and you have to believe it. How badly do you want it? And
how strongly do you believe it? Throughout this book, Wendi
and I have shared stories and outlined steps that have worked for
us and for our teams... but ultimately, *your response is up to you.*

The question is not whether you are capable. *You are!* I can't
tell you how strongly I believe in you. And I can say that because
I've seen this business work for people from every background
and with every personality type you could imagine. The question is whether you are willing to reject excuses and take the
steps needed to succeed. I could have made many excuses, but
I'm so glad I didn't.

Here are some of the excuses that have crossed my mind over the years, especially at the beginning. I've heard them from many others as well. I can tell you without hesitation that *none of these things should stop you.* You have the potential to be wildly successful and to leave a legacy for your family and many others. The things that seem insurmountable now will one day be stories you tell others—stories about how, with a little faith and persistence, you accomplished things that once seemed impossible.

1. *Shy*

Oh my word, was I ever shy! When I was young, my family sang in church a lot. I never wanted to be on stage at all, and certainly not while holding a microphone and singing. But I did, because that's what my family did. My sister Jenni played the piano and sang like an angel. My sister Wendi played the guitar and was always the lead singer because she has an incredible voice and "shy" is not in her vocabulary. (I joke that I didn't even know I could speak until she left for college.) When we did our family concerts, guess what my musical talent was? I was the tambourine player and back-up singer. I had a few solos, but I hated doing it.

Let's be honest: anybody can play the tambourine! Looking back, I love that my parents made me feel special with that darn instrument. I felt so important. And I believe something inside me blossomed each time I played the tambourine on stage. In my teens, my parents made me take modeling classes to help me with confidence.

> The things that seem insurmountable now will one day be stories you tell others.

My mom and I were even once featured in "Teen" magazine for a before-and-after photoshoot.

As an adult, I still struggled with speaking in public. I remember when I was the president of the booster club for my two daughters' cheer teams. I was so shy I couldn't even speak at the parent meetings. The vice-president, who was a friend of mine, had to do all the speaking. Now I can speak at events with a thousand people!

When I decided to start my business, though, I made a choice to believe in myself and to get out of my own way. I had to decide for myself, *I can do this*. Just like playing the tambourine on stage or modeling, I made myself get out of my comfort zone.

It's so worth it! And not just because of the success I've seen in business. The personal development I have experienced over this journey has made me so much happier and more confident. In fact, that inner change is both how and why I am committed to changing more lives. I'm passionate about helping others realize their potential. I've seen that when we are self-focused and when we compare ourselves to others, we hinder our ability to be the best we can be. But when our focus changes from helping *me* to helping *others*, everything changes. Our confidence, our perspective, and our influence grow beyond what we could have believed possible.

2. *Fear*

Wendi talked about it earlier, but I'm going to touch on it here again. *Fear is a liar.* Whatever you are afraid of, face it head on. Just go do it.

I remember being so afraid of going on a zipline in Hawaii. My husband said to me, "Do it! What's the worst that could happen?"

Um, hello? I could die! But I went on the zipline, and clearly I didn't die. It was awesome!

Whatever your fear is, whether it is speaking to people one-on-one, or in a group, or to a large crowd, just *do it.* Make yourself do it. Then do it again. Do it another time. Guess what? Pretty soon, you won't be afraid. You win!

By the way, I went on *nine* ziplines that day! I don't want to do it again, mind you. Ever. But now I know I can do it, and fear can't hold me back.

3. Not good enough

Yes, you are! When I was twenty-two years old, Steve and I moved from Oklahoma to Florida. I had been an administrative assistant for four years for the company I worked for in Oklahoma. Now, starting over in a new state, I found myself intimidated and terrified by the job application process because I didn't have a college degree. I knew I had the experience. I knew I was organized and a go-getter and a thinker. But because I didn't have a degree, I let fear and worry take over.

Don't believe the lie that you aren't enough. You are amazing.

I applied for a secretarial job at a company, and I got the job right away. It was a step down from what I had done prior, but it was a job and I was thankful. I was hired by the administrative assistant at the company, a very sweet lady with a master's degree who had been with the company for several years. I started the job as the office secretary, and honestly, I fell in love with it. I did it very well. I loved answering the phones and helping others. I loved going above and beyond.

A few weeks after I began that job, the owner and the general manager invited me to lunch as a reward for my work. While at lunch, they commended me for being such a hard worker and for being a doer (there is that word again!). Then they told me I would be going back to the office with a new job title. In fact I was going to take the job of the lady who had hired me. When we returned, she was gone, and her desk was empty of her personal things. It was crazy! I felt so sad for her, but I was also so proud of myself. I never should have doubted my abilities or my potential just because my education didn't match some ideal I had in my head.

Don't believe the lie that you aren't enough. You are amazing. Just be who you are. Be the best version of yourself you can be. If you are a worker and a doer, you can accomplish anything you set your mind to.

4. Not a leader

I never knew I was a leader. I knew I was bossy because my sisters and friends had told me so growing up! But a leader? Who knew?

Leadership isn't something only a select few are born to do. There are as many kinds of leaders as there are people. Just be the leader you would want to follow. Do the things you would want someone to do if he or she were leading you. Who do you admire as a leader? Watch them and learn from them. If you only listen to yourself, you will never know more than you know now. Leaders are always learning, and that qualifies them to lead.

5. Busy

I was a stay-at-home mom when I said yes to this opportunity, but that doesn't mean I wasn't busy. I think stay-at-home moms are some of the busiest people on the planet—and if you are one, you probably agree! I was always on the go. I had five kids. One of them was newly adopted from another country, didn't speak English, and was still in diapers. One was in elementary school, another was in high school, and two more were in college. I went on field trips. I did the laundry and cleaned the house. I was involved in Bible studies and other activities. I helped my husband with some of his businesses. Need I go on? I *was busy!*

> People always find the time for what is important to them. What's important to you?

I also know people from countless different professions and occupations who decided to *do this* and to *do it well*. We've shared some of their stories in this book, but there are many more. People always find the time for what is important to them. What's important to you? What do your actions reveal about your values and priorities?

I started saying a long time ago, "Nothing changes if nothing changes." If you want change, you have to start making changes. How you spend your time is important. Don't let the "busy badge" keep you from a life-changing decision!!

6. Pride

I almost let pride stop me! And when I think about that, I kind of freak out. What if I had said no because I was embarrassed to sell skincare? What if I had said no because it was a different kind of business model? What if I had said no because I prided myself on not needing help? I am so thankful I didn't let pride stop me! I could have, but I didn't. I won. I put pride aside, changed my family's life, and now have helped change thousands more. You can, too!

7. Guilt

Do you ever find yourself feeling selfish or even guilty for wanting more? You know others have less than you, so you tell yourself you are fine how you are. Yet something inside you knows you could achieve more.

Contentment has its place, for sure—but don't let guilt stop you from reaching your potential. You were created to succeed and to give. I've often heard it said (and the Bible teaches it, too) that God blesses us so we can be a blessing to others. Complacency or false humility won't help anyone! Think for a moment about how much *more* you could do for *others* if money wasn't an obstacle.

Steve and I have always been givers. No matter what financial scale we were on, we were givers. Sometimes to a fault, if that is possible. And because we said yes to this opportunity, we've been able to do more than we ever dreamed possible. Just the other day, we were driving to our ranch, a beautiful property of over one thousand acres we were able to buy because of our business. The view is breath-taking. We were both in awe. We know we will be able to hold retreats there that will be life-changing for people. Steve said, "Can you believe what God has done? It's incredible!"

It's okay to want to do more! It's not about wanting more money or material things for their own sake. That would be superficial and empty. It's about what money can do. Money is like oxygen— you have to have it! Life is expensive. We have house payments. We have car payments. We have bills. We have college funds for kids. And we have weddings for kids! My daughters got married a year apart. It's not cheap! We were able to pay cash for both, and they had the weddings of their dreams. I am so thankful I was able to bless them that way, and I'm so glad to be able to bless others as well.

> It's not about you—it's about your customers.

Good things cost money. Your favorite charity or foundation. Helping missionaries on the mission field. The church building fund. Adoption and helping others who are adopting. Assisting people in need without having to think, "Can I afford this?" Just think of all the things you could do for your family and for so many others. Don't let guilt stop you!

8. Age

Do you think you are too old? I started in my mid-forties. Now I'm in my fifties. I know successful people in this business in their seventies. Greater age isn't a problem—it's an opportunity! As the people in my circle of influence get older, they need skincare products more than ever. And many of them have more disposable income than they did when they were younger. Maybe you sell a different product, but the principle is the same: don't let your age be a hindrance, because it's not about you—it's about your customers. Find a way to meet their needs, and you'll be successful.

Think you are too young? My daughters, Cassidi and Makenzi, were twenty-one and nineteen when they began in this business. They were both in college at the time. Cassidi was a full-time senior with three jobs (she was a nanny, worked at a church, and also worked at a boutique). Makenzi had started her own business making headbands while in high school, and her headbands were being sold in over fifteen stores in the U.S. as well as through her online store. She worked countless hours each week sewing by hand, shipping her product to customers, advertising, making contacts, and more.

Today, they are both top leaders and earners in the business. They watched me work, and they decided they wanted this kind of financial freedom and time freedom. They didn't want to settle for the "American Dream" that most people think of. Go to college. Get a degree. Work forty-plus hours per week. Live for the weekend. Get a few weeks off each year. Repeat. They wanted more. They wanted something different. They wanted to work for *their dreams*, not someone else's. They decided age didn't matter to them. They knew they'd be successful because they *decided* to be successful. They didn't let anything or anyone put them in a box. And you shouldn't either!

9. *No money to begin*

That is all the more reason to do this! If year after year you are in the same financial situation, maybe it's time to make a change. If you don't try, you'll never know if it could work.

Remember, you can't start *any* business without startup money. It takes money to make money. If you're going to build a business, it's going to take an investment of time, finances, energy, and creativity. Once you've decided to do it, though, you'll be amazed how you are able to find the money to start and to grow your business. And if you run it like a business, it will pay like a business.

How do you find startup money? Get creative! Sell that gold jewelry you never wear anymore. List unneeded furniture on Craigslist. Do some extra work for someone. Stop going out for coffee for a few weeks. Eat at home more often to save money. Evaluate your monthly bills and cancel a subscription or service. Don't buy that new bag right now. Instead, *invest in your future.*

10. *The market is too saturated*

No, it's not! It might feel like that at times, but it's like when you own a certain car, say, a Honda Accord. If you buy an Accord, suddenly you see them everywhere. There really aren't more of them, but you *notice* them more. It may seem like everyone is already in your business, but that's simply not true. No matter how big the company is, it's a drop in the bucket compared to the market, because the market is *everyone*. Plus, people grow up. They enter the job market. They retire. There are always new prospects who need your product or who have money to spend, time to invest, dreams to build.

If you are selling a *consumable* product that *works*, the sky is the limit. People will buy it over and over. A consumable product is smart! Especially if it's a great one. It's built-in job security.

There is room for you, especially if you are passionate about your business and willing to work hard. If you really think too many people are already doing the same business as you, then just do it better!

Actually, the more people who have heard about your product or opportunity, the better, because you don't have to work so hard to convince them of its credibility. There's a good chance they are mostly convinced already, and you get to come along and reap the reward. Rather than assuming they have already decided against it, assume they just need one more nudge to buy your product or sign up on your team.

Remember, you have a unique sphere of influence. That's the beauty of this business model. Wendi and I are sisters with many, many shared contacts, yet we have both built very large teams. Maybe no one is selling to your niche. Or maybe the people in your world already said no to someone else, but they know you. They trust you. They like you. Look at your potential contacts with faith and hope!

11. I don't know anyone

You know more people then you think. And when you start working on expanding your network, you'll be surprised how easy it is to connect with people. Find a group on Facebook. Join a local club. Walk around your neighborhood and actually talk to people. Instead of reading a book at soccer practice, talk to other parents. It's amazing how you can connect to more people when you *try*!

How do I know you can do this? Because I did it. And if I can overcome these obstacles, so can you! There is nothing very special about me. But I'm determined. My yes is yes. I am a thinker and a doer. I wanted change, so I made change. I may not be the lead singer, but I sure am a heck of a tambourine player!

WENDI

This chapter makes me smile because I can see Debbi up there on the church stage playing that tambourine. I can see the red carpet in her bedroom that my mom thought would help her be more outgoing. And I can see her chasing me down the hallway telling me what to do, because she certainly wasn't shy at home!

Honestly, I'm so proud of her, because she was legit *shy*. She was the kid who would hide behind Mom's leg. I couldn't fathom that. I was the kid who, when you walked into our house, jumped up on the pool table with my guitar and started singing you a song. I have always loved being on stage—the more people, the better! So when Debbi asked me to do business with her, the part about talking to people didn't bother me at all. I also didn't overthink what the future would look like or what I needed to do. I figured Debbi would tell me what to do, and I'd do it. She did, and I did, and it worked out great!

If people want to find an excuse, they will.

When I hear people making excuses about why they can't be successful in this business, it makes me laugh. If people want to find an excuse, they will. For example, when I first joined, my sister was already very successful in the business. I could have said I wouldn't be able to be successful because she had already talked to all our family members and mutual friends, but that thought didn't even cross my mind.

I lived in the Nashville, Tennessee area at the time, and there were already many car achievers from our company there. I could have looked at that and said, "There is so much saturation here," but I never did. I just thought, *If they can do it, so can I.*

Remember, right before I started working the business, my family had adopted a sibling set of three. I could have totally used that as an excuse not to work. Have you ever adopted three kids at once? It is a *lot!* Bennet had just turned thirteen, and the twins, Kaleb and Kali, were nine; and we were still adjusting to all the things becoming a family of seven had brought about. I also managed the singing/acting careers of my two oldest kids, Cooper and Gatlin, so I was traveling back and forth from Nashville to Los Angeles for them to audition and work. Along with that, I was a part-time worship leader at my church, I was doing all the bookkeeping for Brian's production company, and I was doing all the normal home chores moms do. I was extremely busy. But I never thought of that as a bad thing. I just knew I needed to make some extra money for my family, so I put my head down and went to work.

I truly didn't care what anyone thought of me. For whatever reason, I just didn't go there in my mind. Once a very close friend of mine told Brian she was going to have to unfriend me on Facebook if I kept posting about my company. She was kidding... sort of. The next time I saw her, I talked to her about it. I told her I had to work to provide for my family and I would love to count on her support. A few months later, she became one of my customers.

People don't know what they don't know, and sometimes, if they aren't familiar with a certain product or business model, they may have preconceived notions about it. If someone is negative with you about your business, don't take it personally.

When you can, explain to them that you love what you're doing, and while they may not want to make a purchase or join you in business, you'd really appreciate their emotional support as you are working to help provide for your family. If someone has a problem with that, they may not be the kind of friend you thought they were.

Once you are able to get past the barriers to *starting* this business and *working* this business, you will be amazed at the results. I'm not just talking about money or a new car or trips to exotic beaches. I'm talking about true life change, both for you and for those on your team. That's what we mean when we talk about leaving a legacy. I truly believe my work is building a legacy that will impact hundreds of thousands of people for good.

We've already talked about several components of this legacy, but as we bring this book to a close, let me sum them up for you.

1. Financial freedom

This is the easiest one to describe, and it's the most urgent need for many people. Financial freedom means not having to live with the stress and burden of debt or the fear of imminent disaster. It means having enough to live well and having enough to share with others. No one can control the future, so no matter what your income is, you still have to trust God, be wise, and work hard. But financial freedom is crucial, and I truly believe it's attainable for all of us.

Not everyone will achieve the same level of income, but everyone can *improve* their level of income. I started out thinking I might earn a few hundred dollars a month to help my family, and that would have been huge. But I ended up transforming our financial picture completely, not only for myself, but for my husband, my children, and thousands of people who later joined my team.

As a family, we have instituted a "one-for-one" giving plan when we make major purchases. That is, when we buy big-ticket items, we find people or families who need the same thing, and we buy it for them. We want our kids to always be aware of people in need around them and to be thinking about how they can help. This giving plan has been a beautiful way for them to see how to live out a "give back" mentality.

> You need money to do things—especially good things. Why not aspire to do as much good as possible?

Because of the way our business has financially blessed us, we have been able to purchase things like cars, braces, and washers and dryers, to pay for college tuitions, to fund adoptions, and even to buy houses for people in need. Debbi came alongside us for a couple of the biggest purchases, and it was so special to be able to do that together. We aren't legalistic about our giving—it's not something we *must* do each time we make a purchase. But it's something we *want* to do whenever we feel led to meet a particular need. Being able to give back on this level has been one of the biggest blessings of our lives.

As Debbi talked about earlier, you need money to *do* things—especially *good* things. Why not aspire to do as much good as possible?

2. Time freedom

The second component of the legacy we are building is time freedom. There is nothing wrong with hard work—I think we've made that clear throughout this book. But no one wants to be the "too busy" parent, the "too busy" spouse, or the "too busy" friend. Time freedom means having the ability to adjust our schedules as needed to do what is genuinely important.

Yes, you'll have to make sacrifices at times, especially at the beginning. You might have to give up some hobbies, lose some free time, wake up earlier, or even miss some events with your kids. You have to make those choices carefully. But keep in mind *any* job requires sacrifices. None of us can do all the fun things or even all the family things we'd like to do. But if you invest your time in your own business, and if you work in a way that produces results, you will discover a level of freedom a nine-to-five job could never offer.

Two incredible, hard-working leaders in this business come to mind: infectious diseases physician Melissa King, MD, and anesthesiologist Panda Korman, MD. Both of these amazing ladies are physicians married to physicians. They know busy. They own that badge! These gals were working seventy to ninety hours a week when they decided to say yes to this opportunity. They believed that growing their network marketing business—in whatever moments they could carve out—was going to lead to the time freedom they were desperate for.

It paid off! Both Melissa and Panda have been able to go part-time in their careers, which is a huge benefit for them and

> Freedom is a better badge than busy.

their families. They worked incredibly hard and achieved the highest title in our company, and because of that sacrificial hard work, they discovered the beauty of living life on their terms. Freedom is a better badge than busy!

3. Satisfaction and fulfillment

A true legacy means living a life worth living, a life that is satisfying, fulfilling, and rewarding. Human beings long for fulfillment. There is something inside us that wants to succeed and to accomplish. That's not a selfish thing. I actually think it's a God thing!

There are many things in life that bring us a certain satisfaction and fulfillment. Finding and being a loving spouse brings satisfaction. Parenting brings satisfaction. Helping others brings satisfaction. And *meaningful work* brings satisfaction. I've seen this over and over in my life and in the people on my team. Work is not bad. It's not a curse. It's an essential part of being human. When you pour your life into something that matters, when you build something that lasts, when you solve problems, when you make a difference, when you see the fruit of your labor—something inside you gets *excited*!

I truly believe you were created and called to build something. I can't tell you exactly what, when, or how, but I think this business could be part of it. But if not, it's something else! Don't settle for a life of just getting by, of simply surviving paycheck to paycheck. Believe you can do something bigger. Dare to leave a legacy.

4. Relationships

I left this one for last because I think it's the most important. People are always more important than money, and this business is about *people* through and through.

Building amazing new friendships is one thing about this business I didn't see coming. In the past five years I've made some of the best friendships of my life, all because I said yes to this opportunity. One of the most fabulous people I've met is my friend, Jessica Bettencourt. She was introduced to me by a mutual friend, and I had the privilege of doing the conference call that brought her into the business. I was also honored to go to Ohio for her business launch and to talk to a room full of her friends. It was one of the best business launches I've ever been part of. I could tell Jessica was greatly loved by the people who came out to support her.

> It's never too early or too late to start building a legacy.

I didn't know her then, but now that I do know her, I understand why. Jessica is a stellar person! She didn't need a new business venture. She didn't need more income. She said yes to this opportunity because she wanted new skincare that actually worked. She very naturally began telling her friends about the products, and the business fell into place. When it did, she and her husband, Mike, decided to give 100% of the profits from their first year of business to the charities they support. *One. Hundred. Percent.* That's incredible! Since that first year, they have continued to give a sizeable portion of their income to charities and missions.

I've watched as Jessica has been a part of funding multiple adoptions, and I've seen the generous spirit in her light up a room as she talks about those sweet children who now have forever families. Our team includes *so many* adoptive families. It's crazy. We have watched in amazement as this business has been a true vehicle for life-changing events.

What I didn't know at the beginning of our adventure together was Jessica had always had it in her heart to adopt, but her husband, Mike, wasn't quite sure. As Mike saw all these awesome adoptions taking place, though, his heart was drawn to adoption. Today, Jessica and Mike have added a precious little girl from China to their beautiful family.

To be honest, I don't know if their adoption (or so many other adoptions) would have happened without this business vehicle. Yes, God could have decided to orchestrate another way. But the reality is *this* was the way they happened. They happened because Jessica said yes to an opportunity and then worked hard so it could change people's lives.

One of the best things I've done with Jessica was an event tour she and I did alongside Debbi and our friend, JoDee, whom I talked about earlier. We called the event "Four Stories," and we traveled to multiple cities, telling the stories about how this business vehicle was changing our lives. I loved every minute with those incredible ladies. I was so proud of each one of them every time they stood up to tell their stories. I shed tears of joy when Jessica talked about the children who had found homes, and I nodded in agreement when she said, "Our success is your potential." I smiled as I watched my sweet sister, who used to be so shy, stand in front of a packed-out room talking about rainbows and unicorns and how her one yes began a series of yeses that has changed thousands of lives. I cried as JoDee talked about the dream she and her husband, Jonathan, had of opening up a place to employ the intellectually disabled and how their giant dream had come to fruition because of this business. I laughed as I told everyone how I used to wash my face with any random bar of soap, never imagining I would one day sell skincare and earn a seven-digit annual income.

It's never too early or too late to start building a legacy. The beautiful thing about a legacy is that it is bigger than any one person. It outlives and out-gives the person who started it. It transcends just "making ends meet" or achieving some level of fame or celebrity. Legacy is about being a blessing to others. You can succeed, and through your success, good things will come to many people.

Conclusion

Can We Leave You
with a Final Thought?

This book is our unique journey. We have loved writing it, and we thank you for reading it. It doesn't stop with us, though. Someday, we're going to hear *your* story, and we're looking forward to reading *your* book. Our success is part of your success; our story leads into your story.

There is nothing that unique about the two of us. We aren't superheroes or freaks of nature. I hope we've made that clear through our stories. We've been transparent with our weaknesses, and we've shared our values and strategies. Honestly, we're just two girls who decided to say yes and to work hard. And along the way, we've had a lot of fun!

When everything is said and done, success isn't measured in how many people you have in your downline, what level you've reached in your company, or how many digits are in your income. Those things are a means to an end, but not an end in itself. What does success look like? It's a word we talked about in the final chapter: *legacy*.

Legacy refers to what we leave behind. It means we lived our life well, we used what was given to us faithfully, and we made the world a better place.

But just because a legacy is something you leave behind doesn't mean it's way off in the future. Your legacy begins now because it is built on who you are. It is built on who you help, what you give, and how you love. What you do right now matters.

The opportunities are out there. God is sending you the boat you need. Now it's up to you. Live your life and leave a legacy!

Acknowledgements

We owe a debt of gratitude to many who have helped us along the way, and to all of you, a huge *thank you*. We want to specifically thank our children and our sweet husbands for being supportive and understanding of the time we've spent pouring into our businesses and this book. We'd also like to give a special shoutout to our dad, whom we admire greatly and love with all our hearts. And to God, the giver of *all* good things.

Also we want to add a *ginormous* thank you to our editor, Justin Jaquith. There is absolutely no way we could have done this book without him. None whatsoever. Thank you for sticking with us through all the crazy and for being so kind and encouraging through this entire process. In our opinion you are the best editor *ever*!

End Notes

CHAPTER 1 /// Smith, Annette. *The Story Factor: Inspiration, Influence, and Persuasion through the Art of Storytelling.* Basic Books, 2006

CHAPTER 2 /// Family of Amelia Earhart. "Quotes by Amelia Earhart." Ameliaearhart.com. Accessed August 20, 2018. https://www.ameliaearhart.com/quotes/.

CHAPTER 3 /// Bush, Lori. Quoted at a corporate event and noted by the authors. Used with permission.

CHAPTER 4 /// *Entrepreneur Magazine.* Facebook, January 19, 2006. Facebook.com. Accessed August 20, 2018. https://www.facebook.com/EntMagazine/posts/%22dear-optimist-pessimist-and-realist/10153900836708896/

CHAPTER 5 /// Ziglar, Zig. *Secrets of Closing the Sale: Updated.* MJF Books, 2012.
/// Goodreads. "Elsie De Wolfe Quotes." Goodreads.com. Accessed August 28, 2018. https://www.goodreads.com/author/quotes/197889.Elsie_De_Wolfe

CHAPTER 6 /// *Stanford News.* "'You've Got to Find What You Love,' Jobs Says." Stanford.edu. Accessed August 20, 2018. https://news.stanford.edu/news/2005/june15/jobs-061505. html.
/// Rodan, Dr. Katie. Quoted during speaking engagements and noted by the authors.

CHAPTER 7 /// Hyatt, Michael. "The Most Powerful Leadership Tool You Have Is Your Own Personal Example." Michaelhyatt.com. Accessed August 20, 2018. https:// michaelhyatt.com/photos/powerful-leadership-tool-personal-example-john-wooden/

CHAPTER 8 /// Adrain, Lorne. A., comp. *The Most Important Thing I Know: Life Lessons from Colin Powell, Stephen Covey, Maya Angleou and Over 75 Other Eminent Individuals.* New York: Cader Books, 1997.
/// Stanley, Andy. *The Next Generation Leader.* New York: Multnomah Books, 2003.

CHAPTER 9 /// *The Holy Bible: New International Version.* "Gospel of Luke, 6:13." Grand Rapids, MI: Zondervan, 2011.

CHAPTER 10 /// Maxwell, John C. *The 21 Irrefutable Laws of Leadership: Follow Them and People Will Follow You.* Nashville, Tenn.: Thomas Nelson, 2007.

Daily Challenges

Here are sample challenges (in no particular order) that you can use with your team. We call them daily challenges because most of them can be completed in one day; we usually post one or more a week to our teams. We find people love doing these, even though they are forced to get out of their comfort zone a bit (which is the point!). They are also great team-building exercises because people encourage and celebrate each other along the way.

Don't be shy about holding people accountable. If they truly want to grow, they will welcome your involvement and feedback. We always have people comment back once they've completed a challenge, which is so encouraging for everyone. At times we've created specific groups for people (such as our direct contacts) who want to join us for an intense thirty-day or sixty-day series of challenges with a super special prize at the end (such as a night away at a great hotel and a spa day the next day).

Of course, you should be doing these too! People learn best by watching you.

1. Define your why. Write a paragraph or list detailing why you are in this business and what your dream is.
2. Have a conversation with a stranger today and get their contact information for follow-up.

3. List five goals you want to reach this month.
4. Find a power partner (accountability partner). Share your goals and invite the person to ask you every month how you're doing in your business.
5. Listen to three training calls.
6. Do a three-way call with your sponsor or one of your directs.
7. Order business cards for yourself. (Check your company's policies regarding this).
8. Host a launch party for at least one direct.
9. Host an event for yourself.
10. List ten people you plan to give product to for birthdays or Christmas gifts.
11. Post a video to your personal Facebook page of yourself discussing your favorite product (one to two minutes max).
12. Post a video to your team Facebook page encouraging and motivating your team (one to two minutes max).
13. Brainstorm one hundred people you have not yet told about your business.
14. Send thirty messages.
15. Make three phone calls. Leaving messages doesn't count!
16. Make sure automatic product replenishment is turned on.
17. Create a challenge or contest for your team—with a prize!
18. Create a Bingo-type card with daily challenges or products to sell for your team. First person to cross out a line (or the entire card) wins a prize.
19. Write a welcome letter to pin at the top of your team page for new consultants.
20. Post a "keep it simple" reminder to your page. Remind people to do the basics every day.
21. Post your success story and picture on your team page and personal page.

22. Add twenty Facebook friends.
23. Read (or reread) your company's code of ethics and policies and procedures files. Then make sure they are available for your team to read as well.
24. Join a new Facebook group focused on a hobby or interest you have.
25. Post to your personal page twice a day, every day, this week.
26. Go to a corporate meeting if there is one near you ("near" is within four hours of driving!).
27. Share three different opportunity calls with prospects.
28. Schedule a Facebook Live meeting for your team.
29. Send an encouraging message to every one of your direct contacts (a personal message, not a group message). If you'd like, pray for them by name while you are at it...or at least think happy thoughts about them ☺ Everyone needs encouragement.
30. Make a "chicken list" of people you would probably tend to avoid for some reason. Then talk to or message five of them. Get out of your comfort zone!
31. Talk to ten people who tell you no. That's right, *no*. Get comfortable with being told no. It's not a bad thing!
32. Schedule a "power hour" with your team where everyone completes as many challenges as possible in one hour. Give a twenty-dollar Starbucks card or some other prize to the winner.
33. Create a copy-and-paste post for your team.
34. Purchase and use one new product yourself.
35. Reach back out to five people who have told you no in the past.
36. Set up a coffee date or other in-person meeting with a new potential customer or team member.

Team Resources
How to Find Contacts

Your relationships are your key to recruiting potential customers and team members. When you stop to think about it, you will be amazed how many people you know! Below are general categories of people in your life. Read through the list and make a note of people who come to mind right now. Every month or so, come back and revisit the list. You'll always think of new names.

Remember each of these people has their own circle of relationships. Even if you get a "no" from some of them, you can often ask them to refer their friends and family to you.

Family: parents, siblings, children, grandparents, cousins, nieces and nephews, extended family, in-laws

Friends and acquaintances: close friends, casual friends, friends you've lost touch with, people you met at social functions such as weddings, people you met on Facebook, neighbors (past and present), classmates, carpool

Contacts on your phone or computer: cell phone contacts, email contacts, WhatsApp, Facebook Messenger, iMessage

Social media networks: Facebook friends, Facebook special interest groups, Instagram followers, Twitter followers, LinkedIn contacts

Lists you already have: Christmas card list, family newsletter list, wedding list, birthdays, alumni association

Work: bosses, coworkers, employees, providers, vendors, customers

Leisure and health activities: gym, health club, sports, hobbies, book club, Toastmasters, sightseeing or tour groups, special interest clubs, social events such as weddings, parties, nights out with friends

Religious or non-profit activities: church, charities, volunteering, missions trips, social justice work

Strangers: people next to you on the airplane, people you see every day but have never met, people you admire and want to learn from, people you think you could help, people you meet on vacation, people whose paths have randomly crossed yours

Contacts through your kids: other parents, teachers, after-school activities, coaches, tutors, carpool, PTA meetings

Professionals you visit: doctors, orthodontists, salon workers, hair stylists, mechanics, massage therapists, lawyers, psychologists, therapists, estate planners, financial advisers

People whose services you use: real estate agents, electricians, plumbers, caterers, house cleaning services, landscapers, music teachers, carpenters, air conditioner technicians, cable TV repair technicians, photographers, web designers, interior decorators, car salespeople, furniture salespeople, servers, mail delivery workers, taxi drivers

About the Authors

Debbi Coder and Wendi Green are sisters, but they share more than just DNA: they are both highly successful sales consultants in the direct selling channel. Debbi began working in the industry in 2012 and Wendi in 2013, and within six months each had risen to the top 2% of their company. Today Debbi's downline has exceeded 80,000 and Wendi's has exceeded 65,000, and they are growing exponentially. Both hold the highest title that exists in their company.

Debbi and Wendi are sought-after speakers and trainers whose experience, success, and communication skills have helped countless people start or grow their multi-level marketing businesses. They are passionate about empowering others to develop the financial freedom, time freedom, personal fulfillment, and genuine friendships they have discovered through their business.

Debbi lives in Tulsa, Oklahoma with her husband, Steve. She has five children: Cassidi and her husband, Taylor; Makenzi and her husband, Drew; Kason and his wife, Payton; and Kyler and Crew; along with her grandchildren: Charleston, Tripp, and baby Hillenburg (on the way). She loves to spend time with her family, travel, mentor her team, and help others be their best.

Wendi lives in Los Angeles, California with her husband, Brian. They have five children: Cooper and his wife, Megan; Gatlin and her husband, Austin; and Bennet, Kaleb, and Kali. Wendi also owns a production company called Jeenyus Entertainment, manages her two oldest children's singing and acting careers, and is passionate about creating wholesome projects in the entertainment industry.

11758167R00092

Made in the USA
Lexington, KY
15 October 2018